Toddler Coloring Book Trucks

Fun Truck Coloring Book Designed Especially For Toddlers

SUNNY HAPPY KIDS

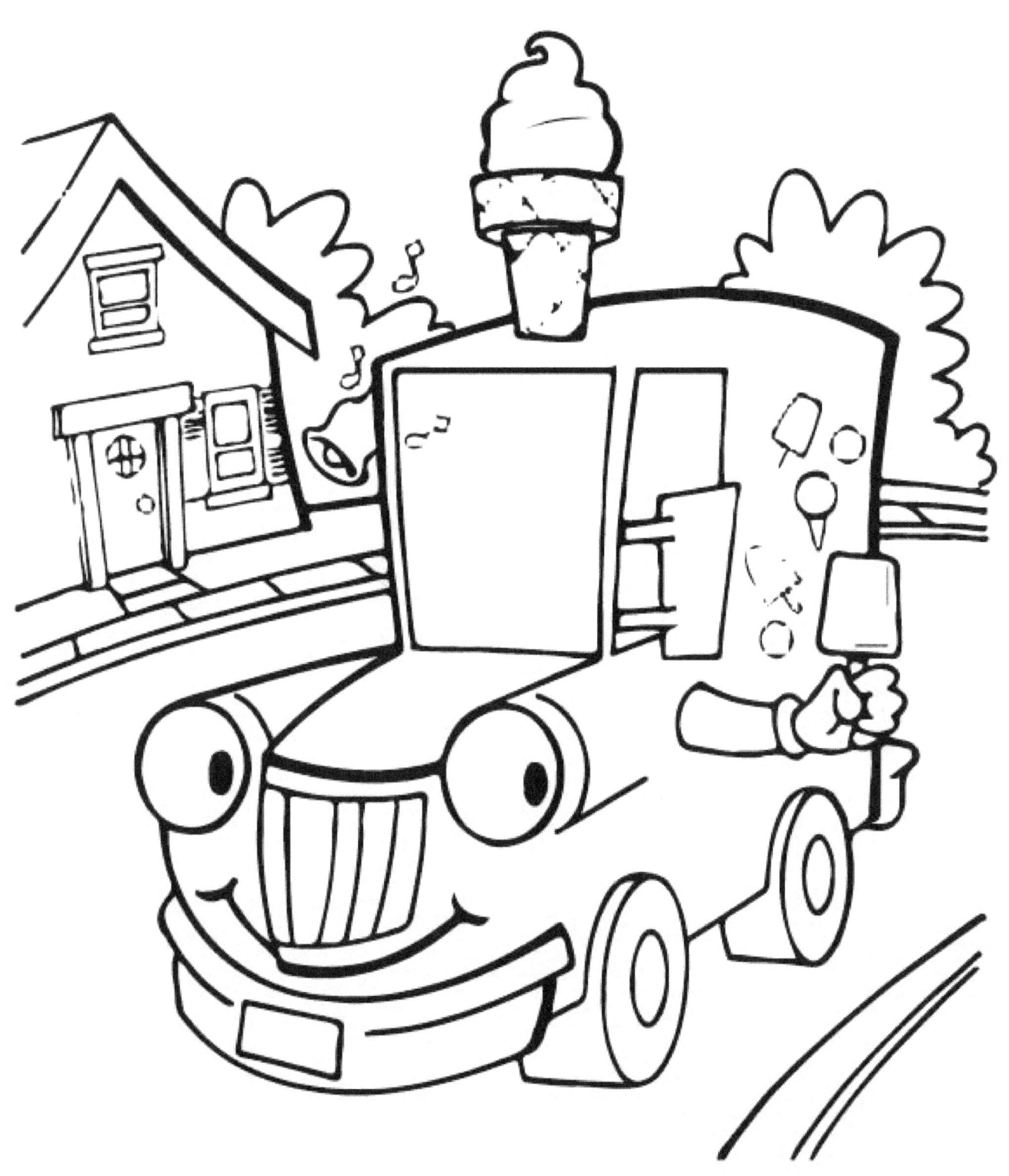

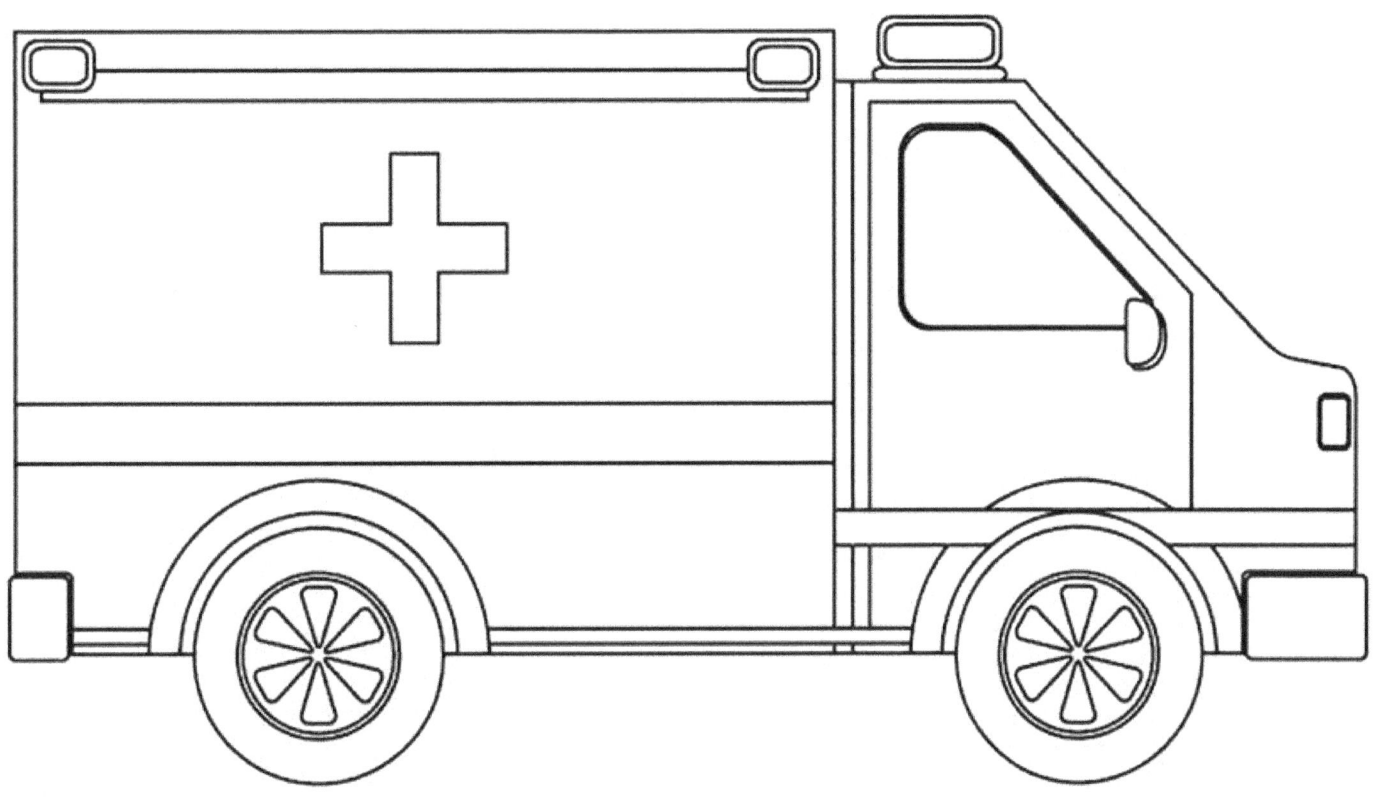

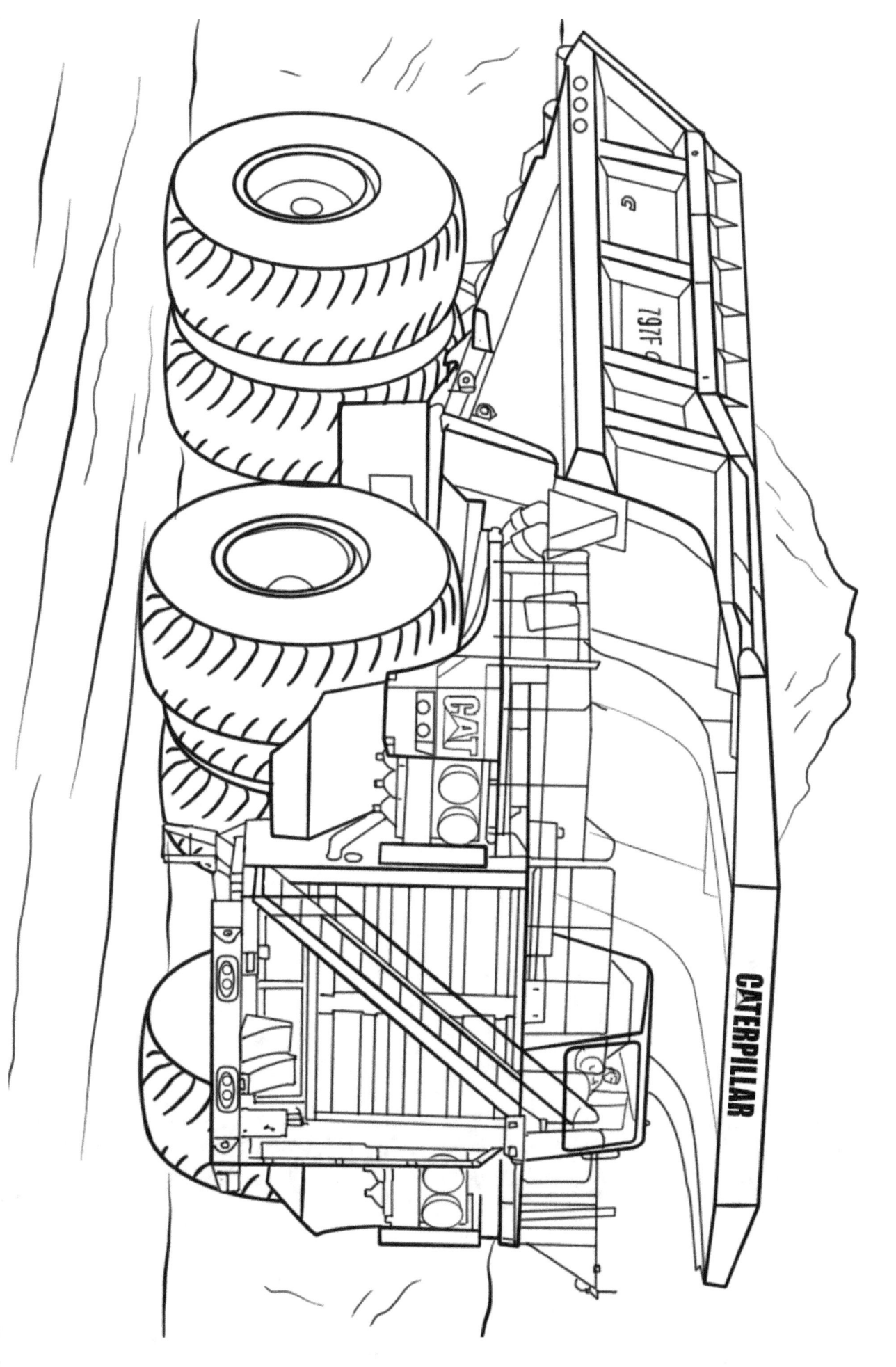

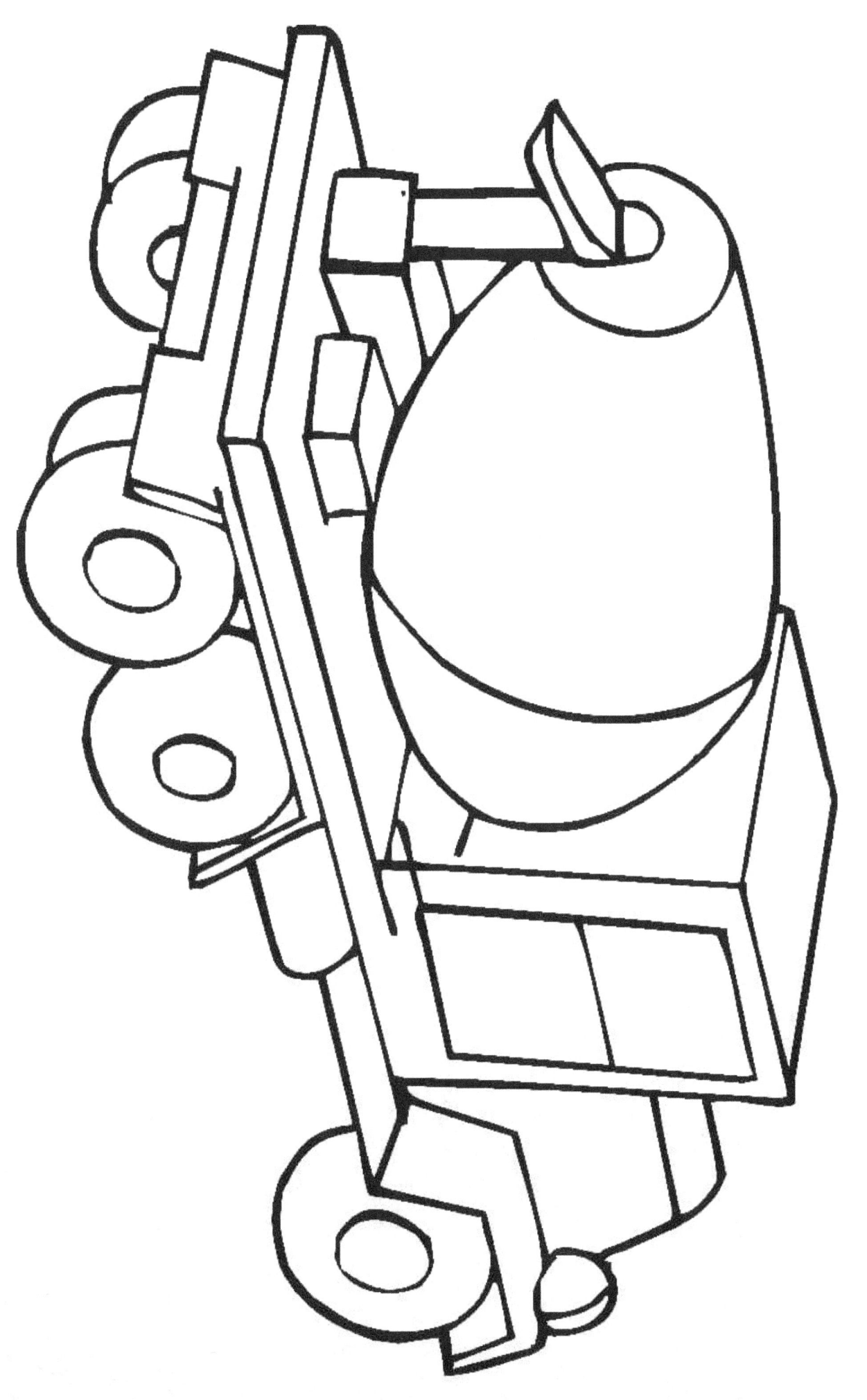

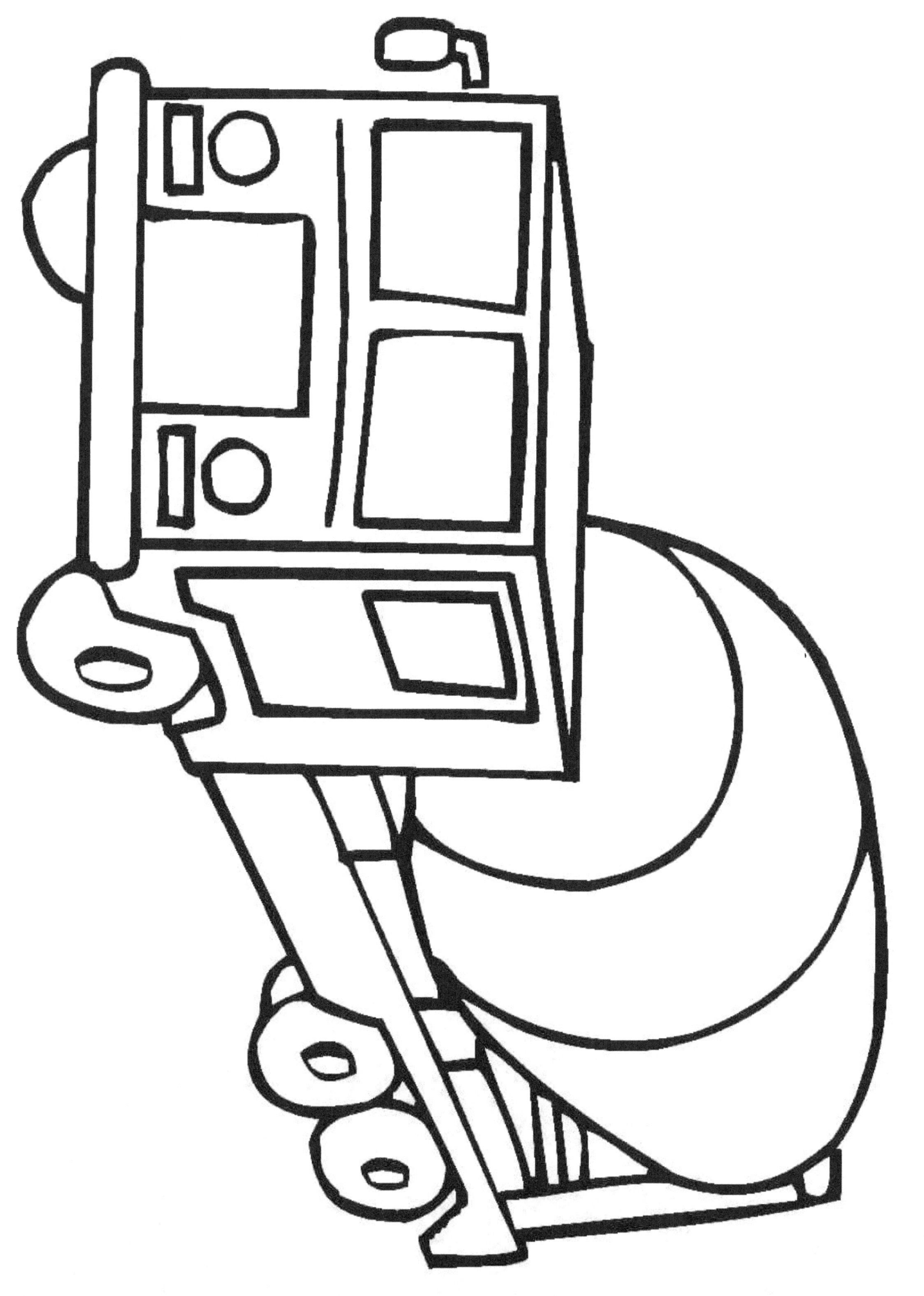

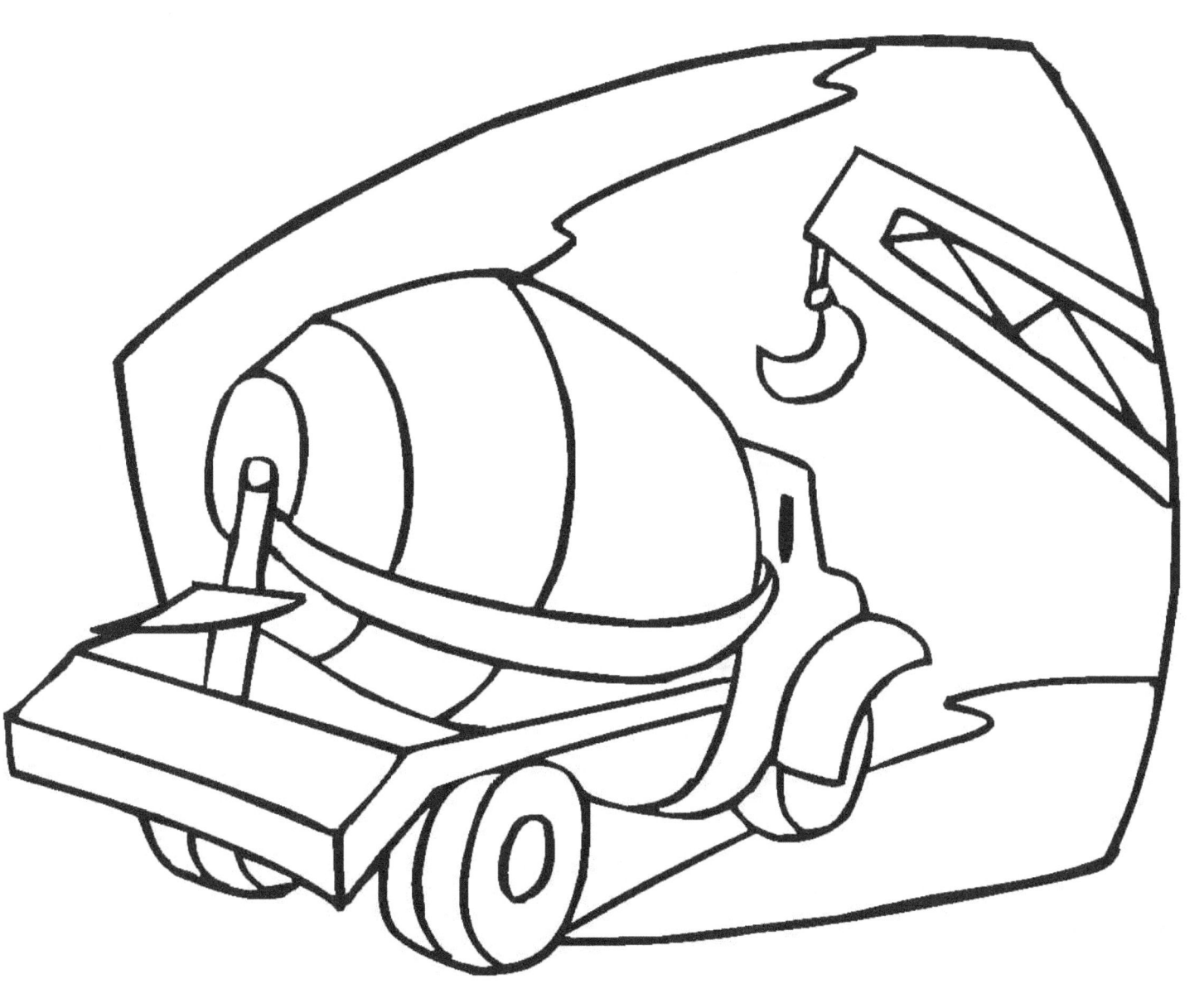

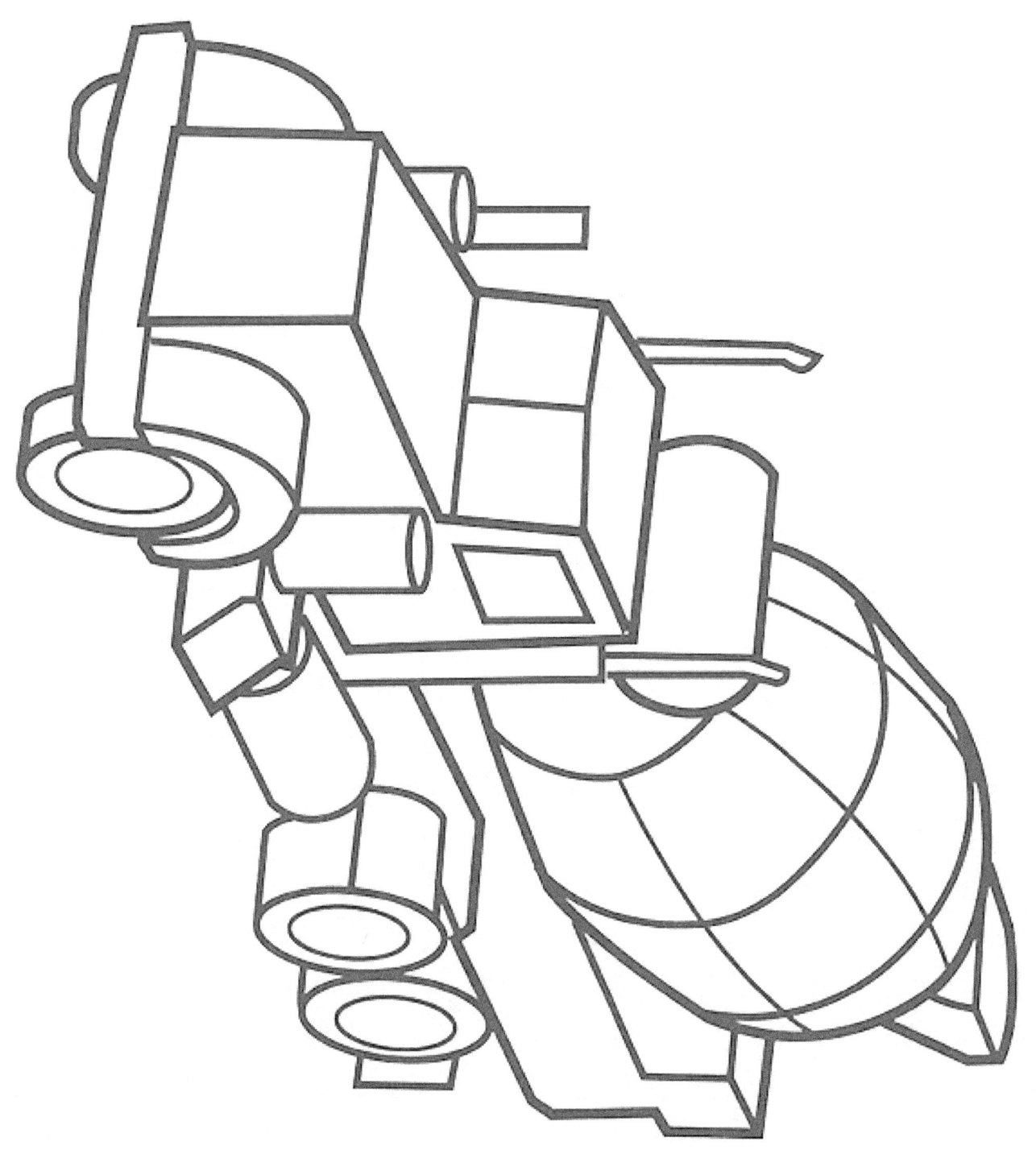

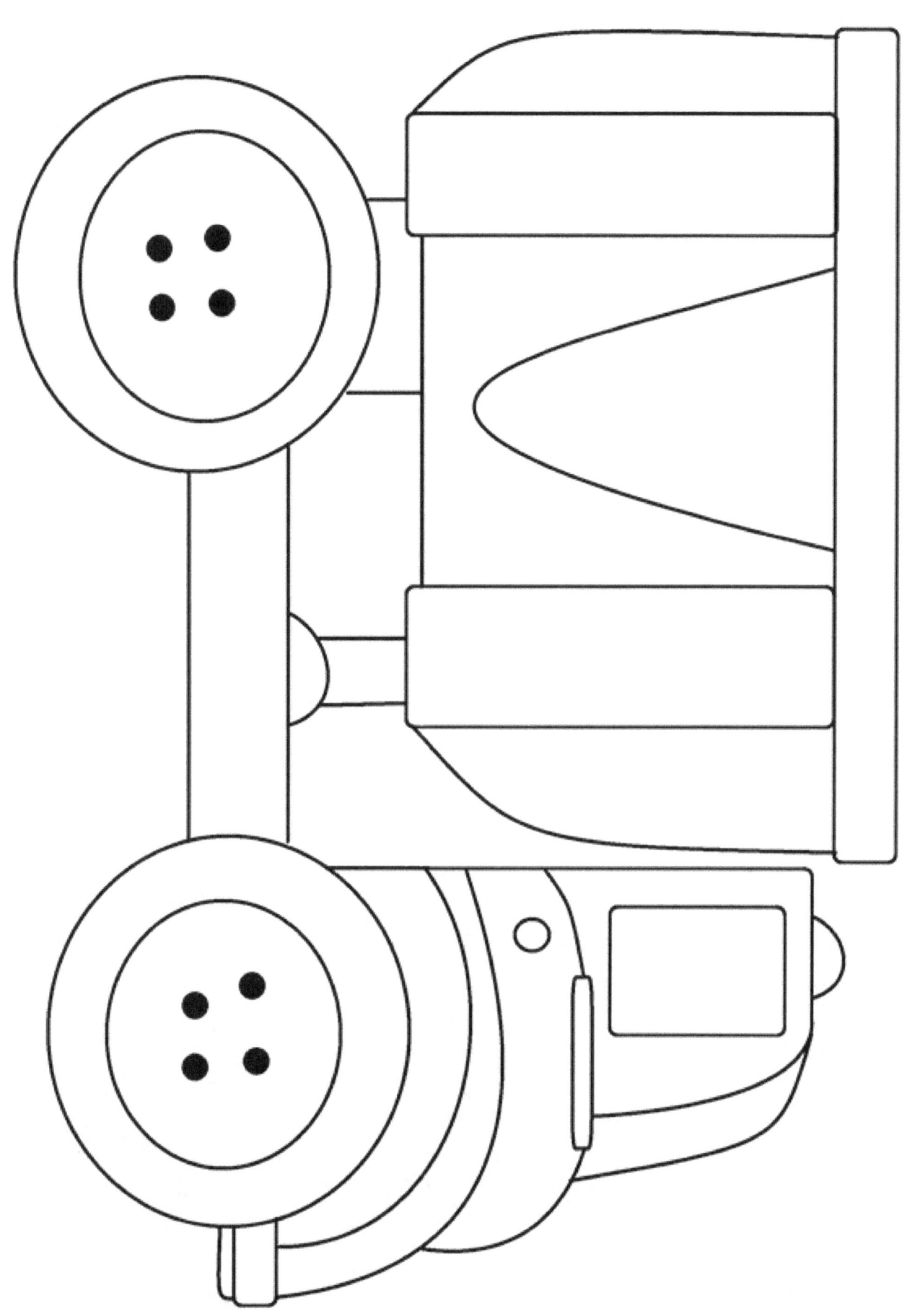

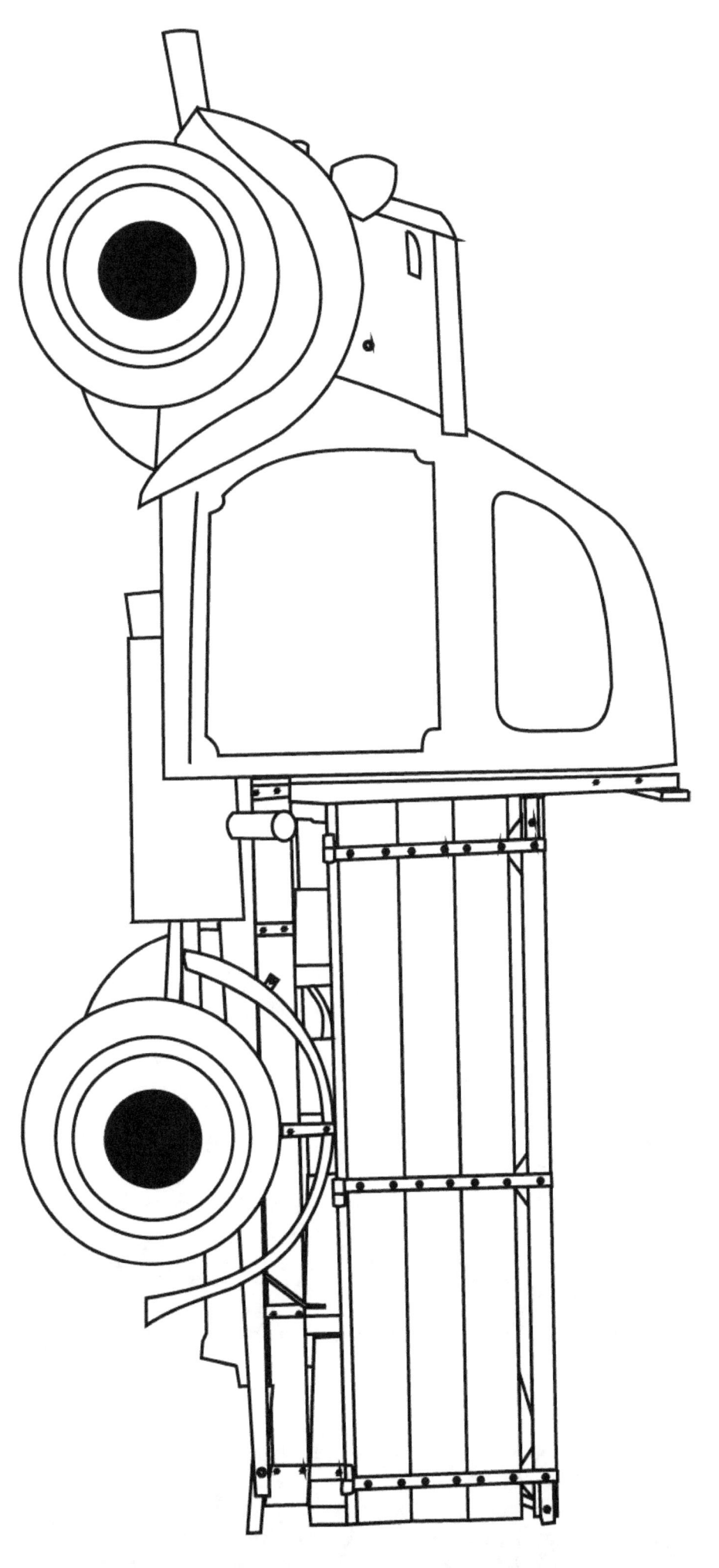

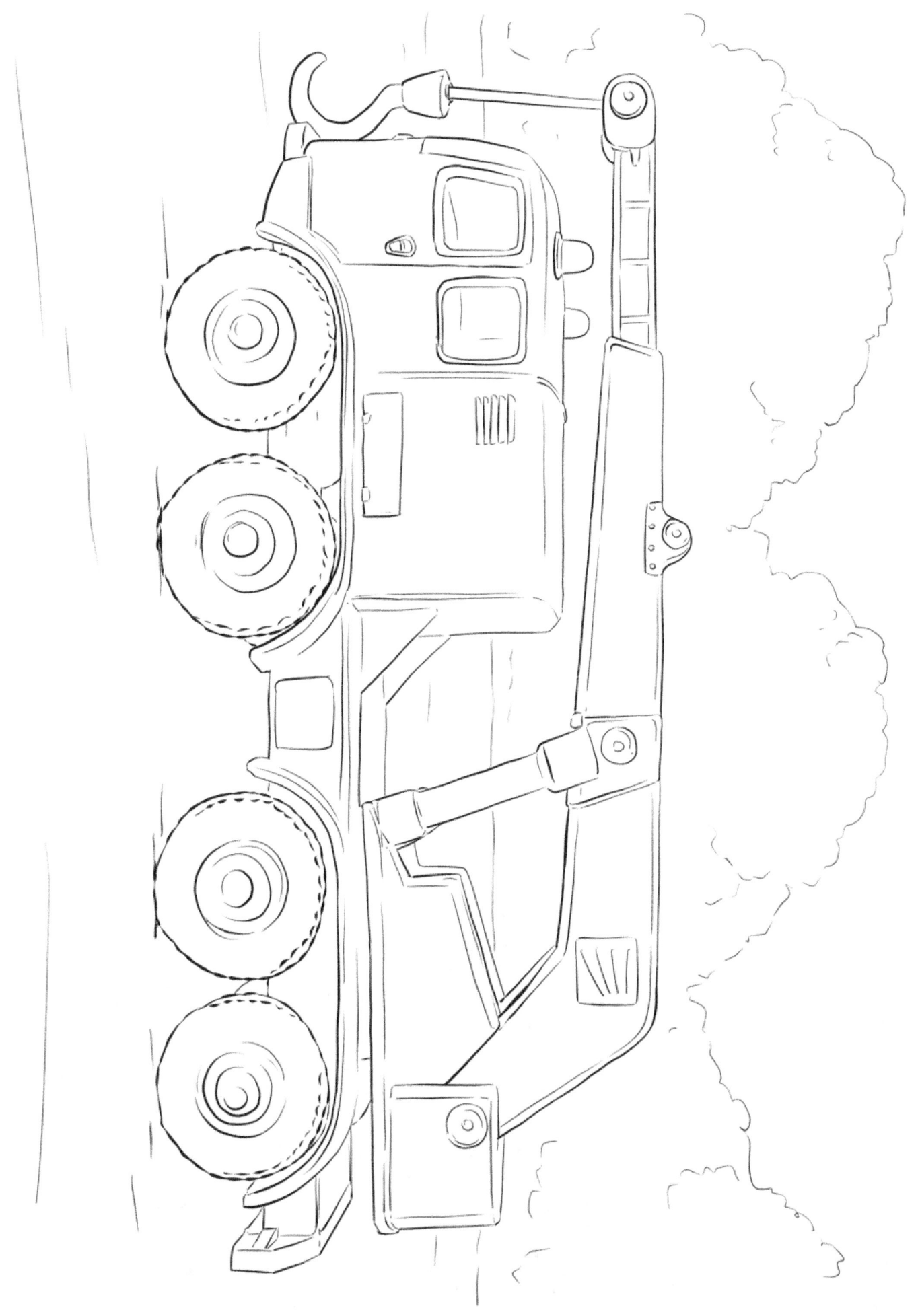

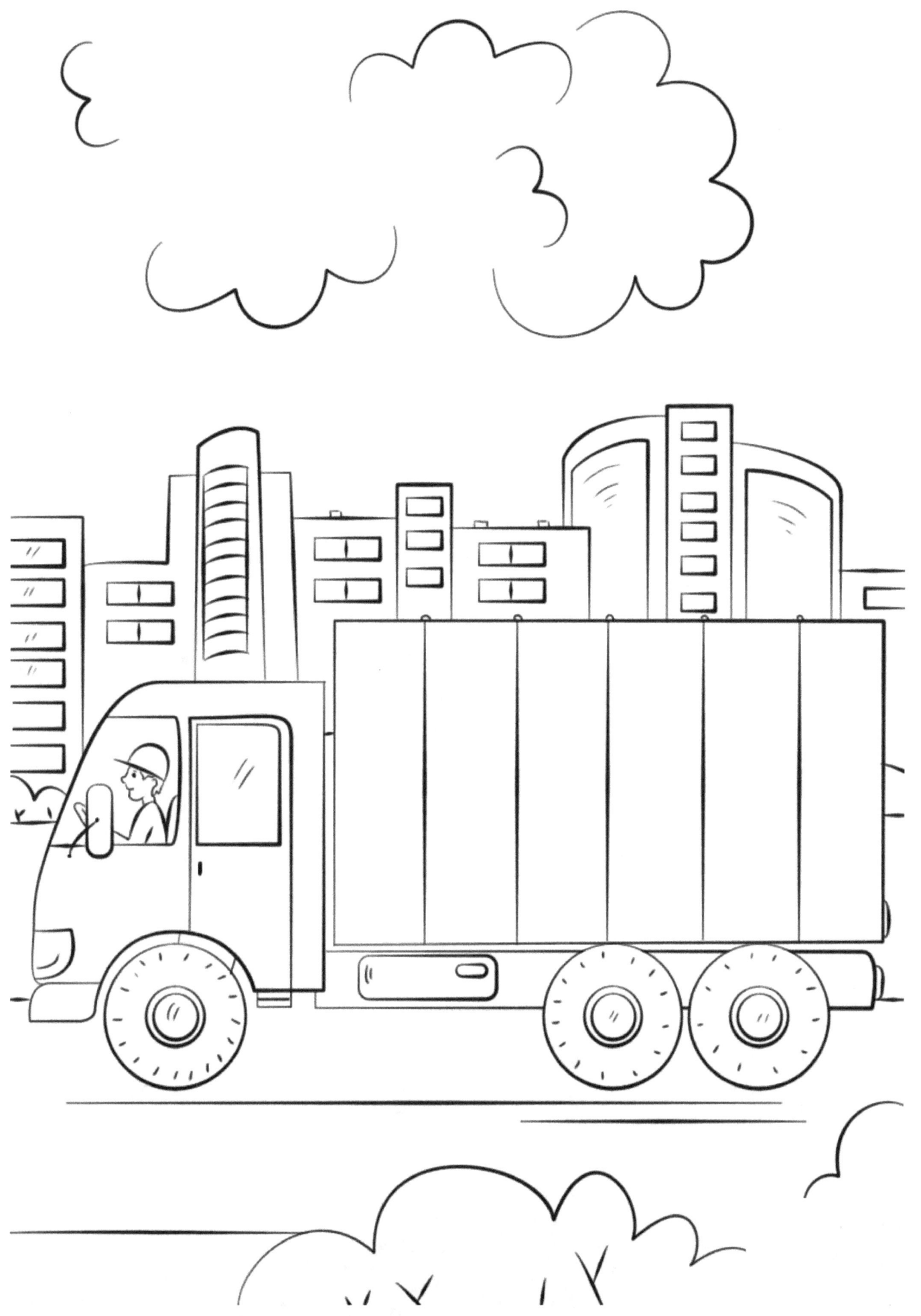

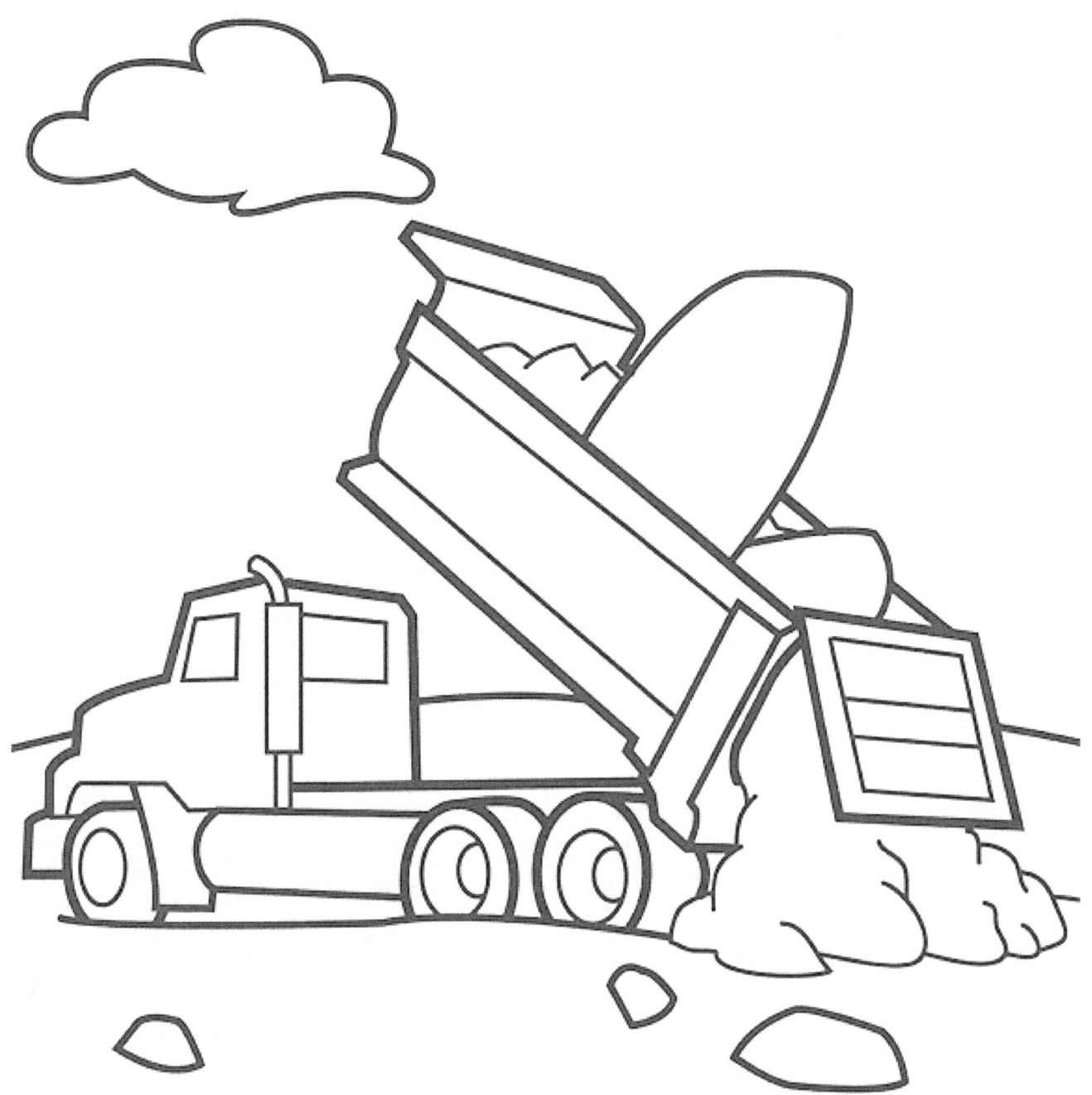

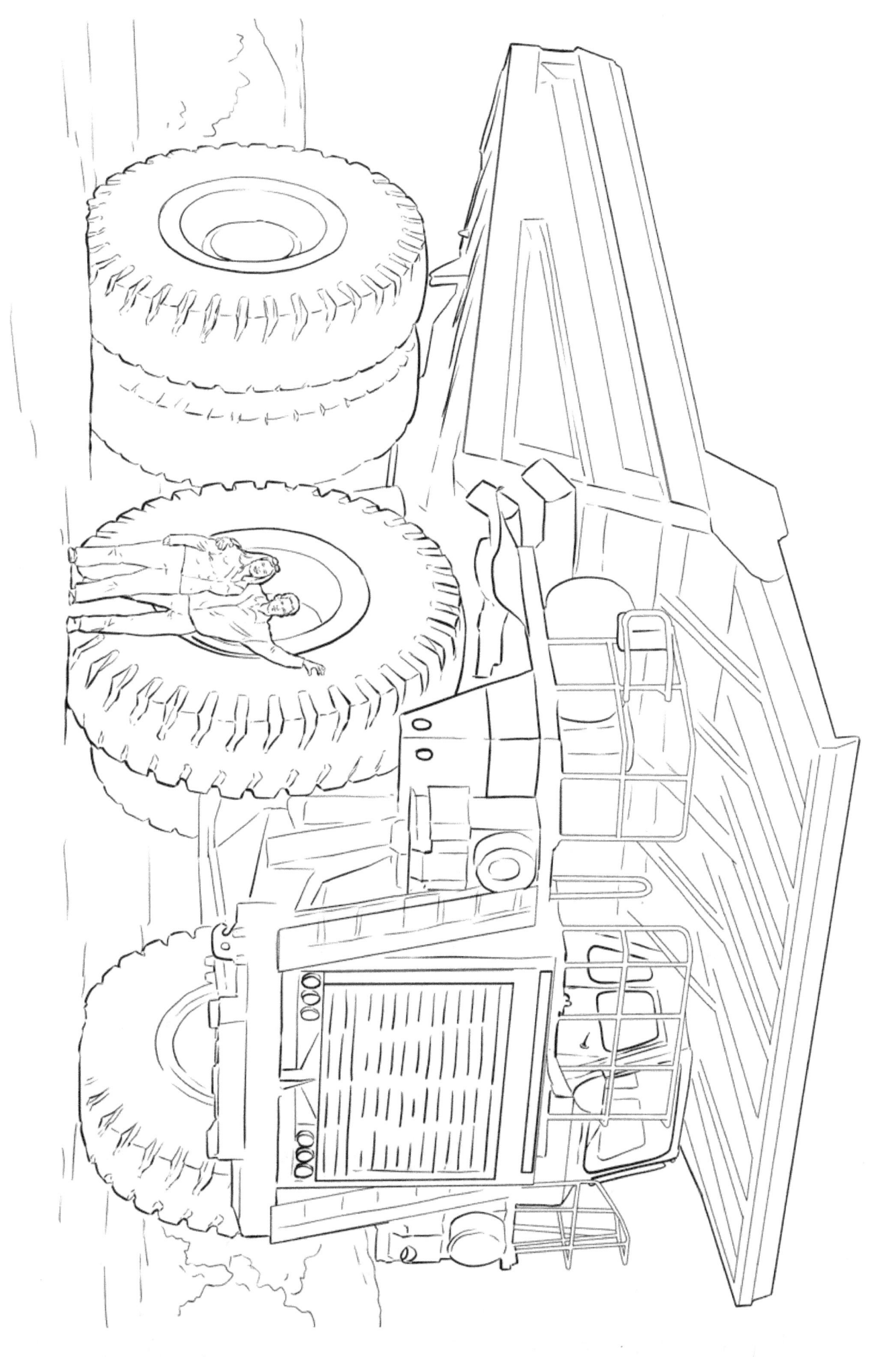

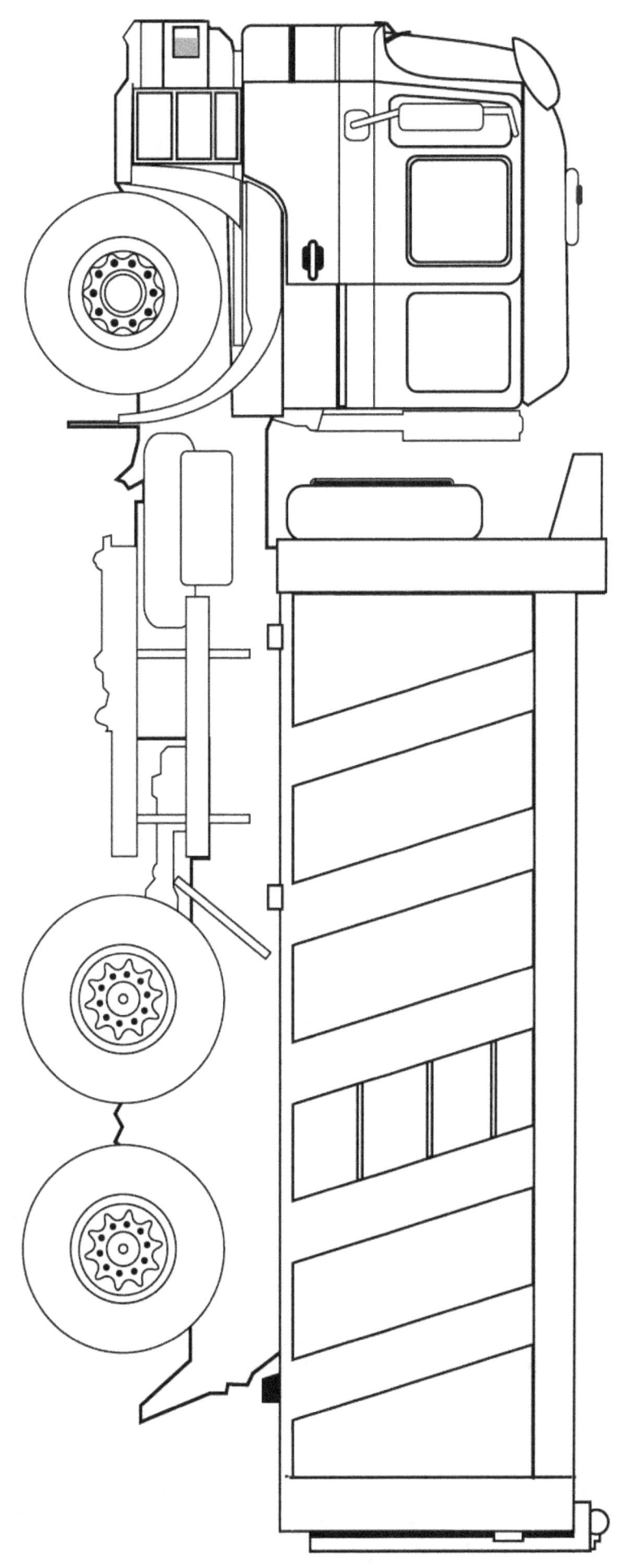

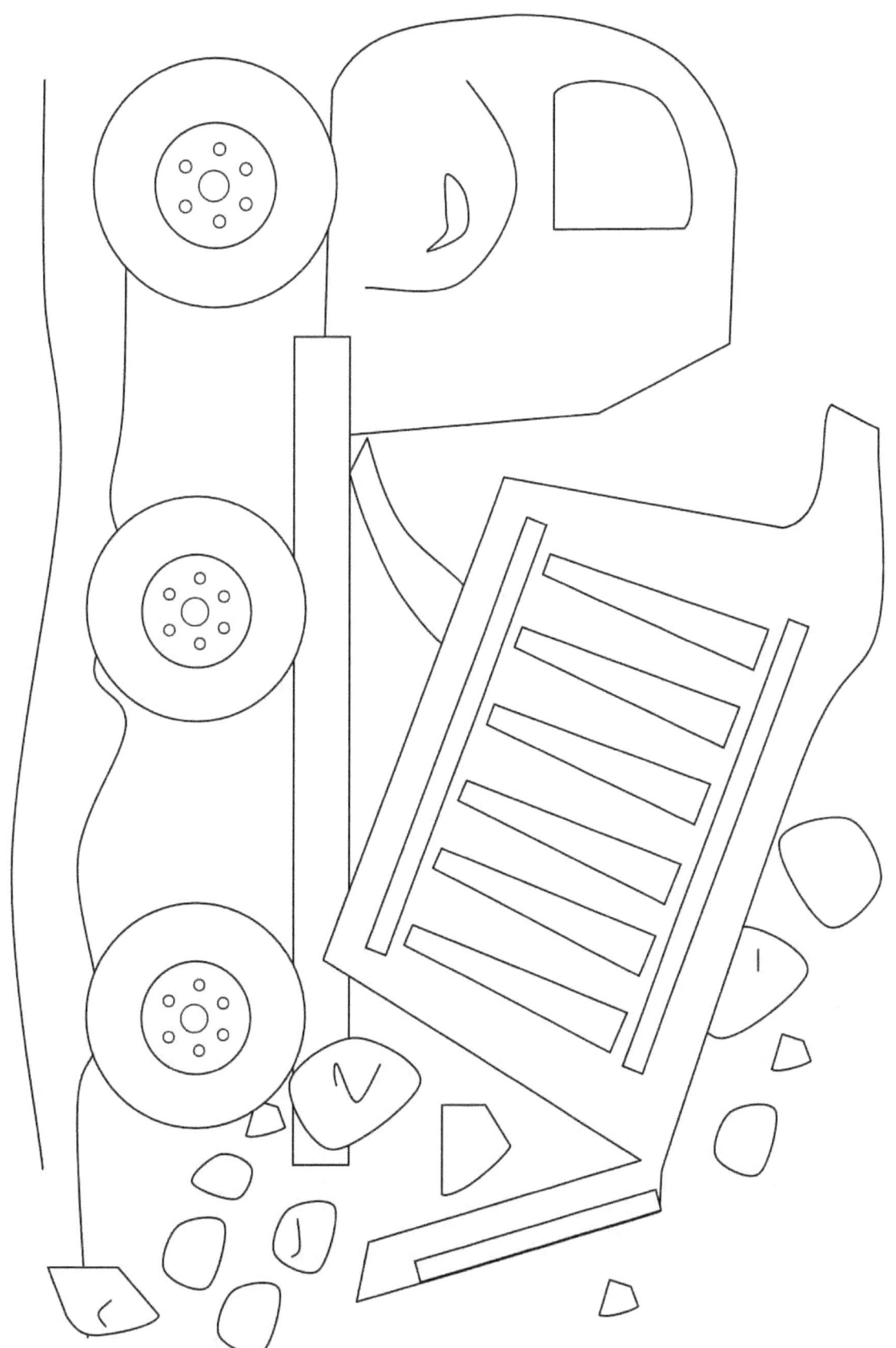

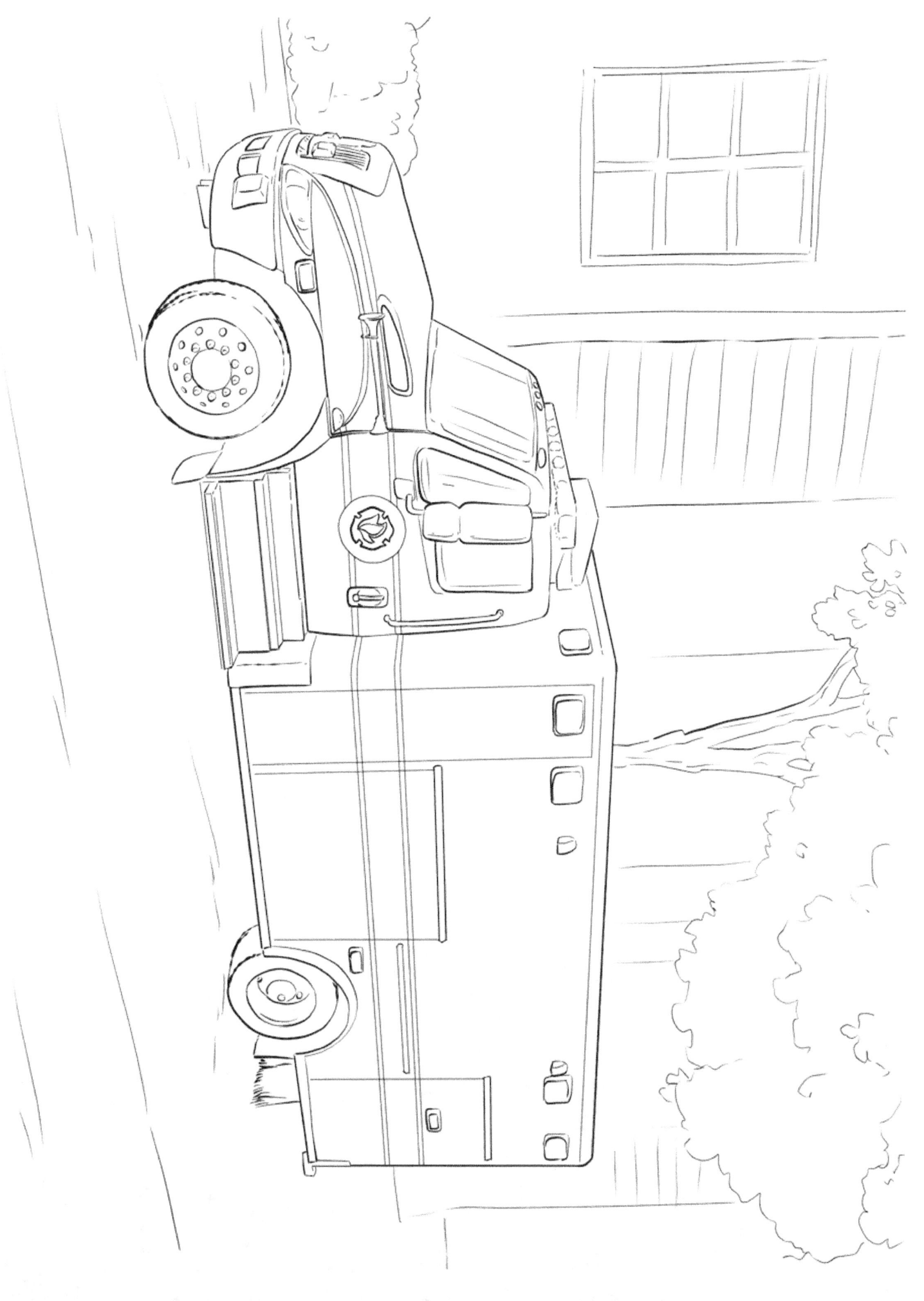

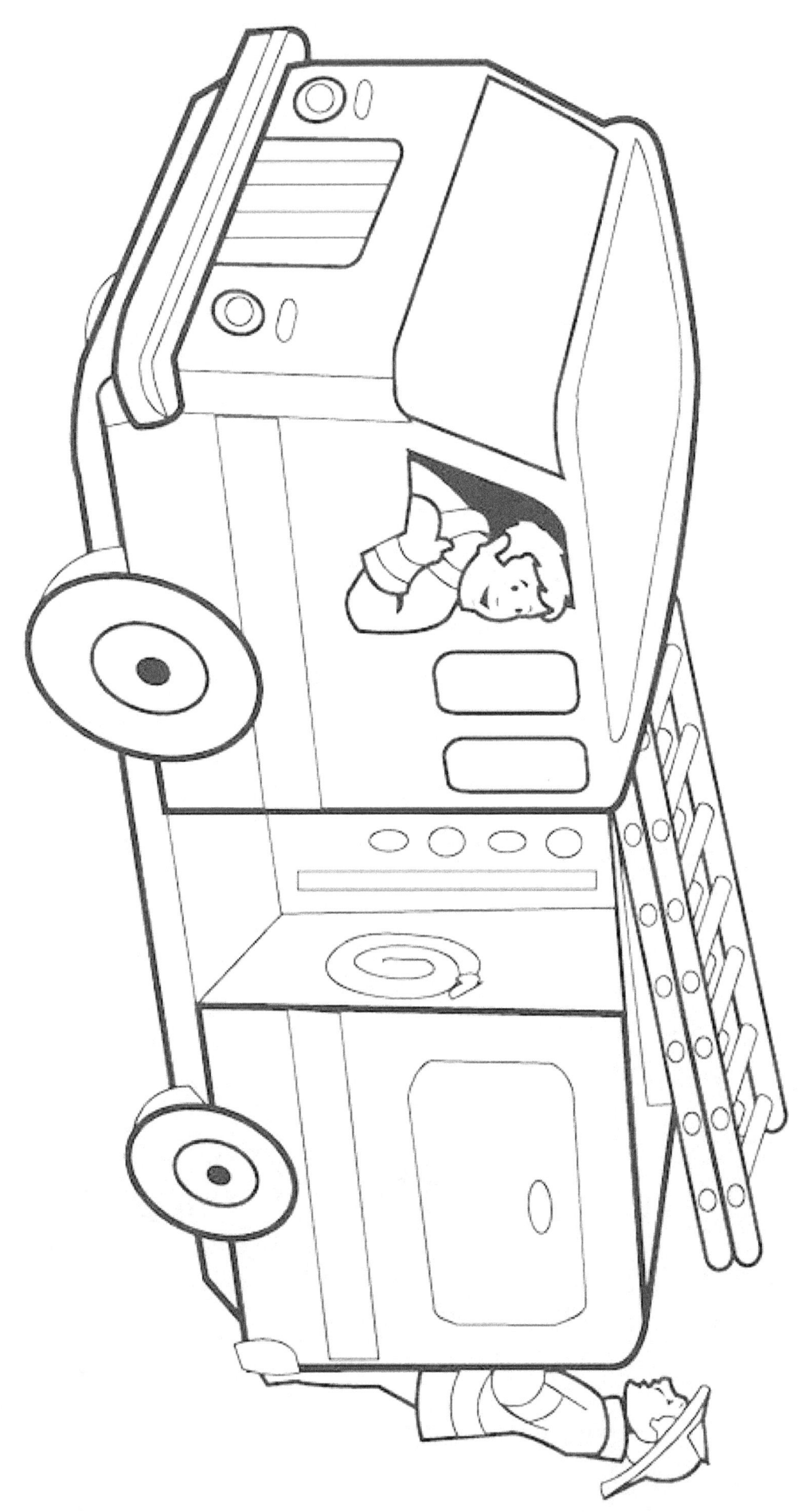

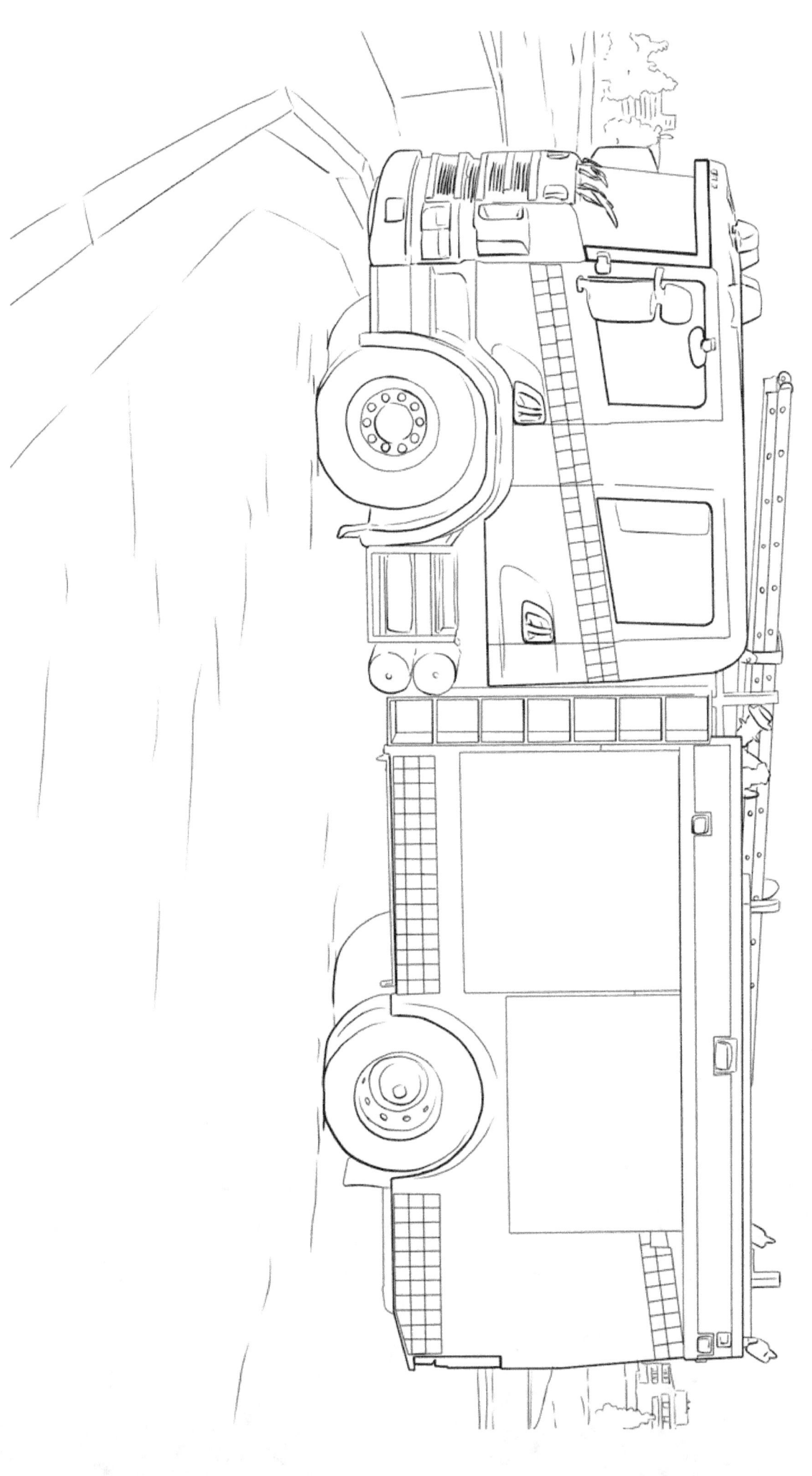

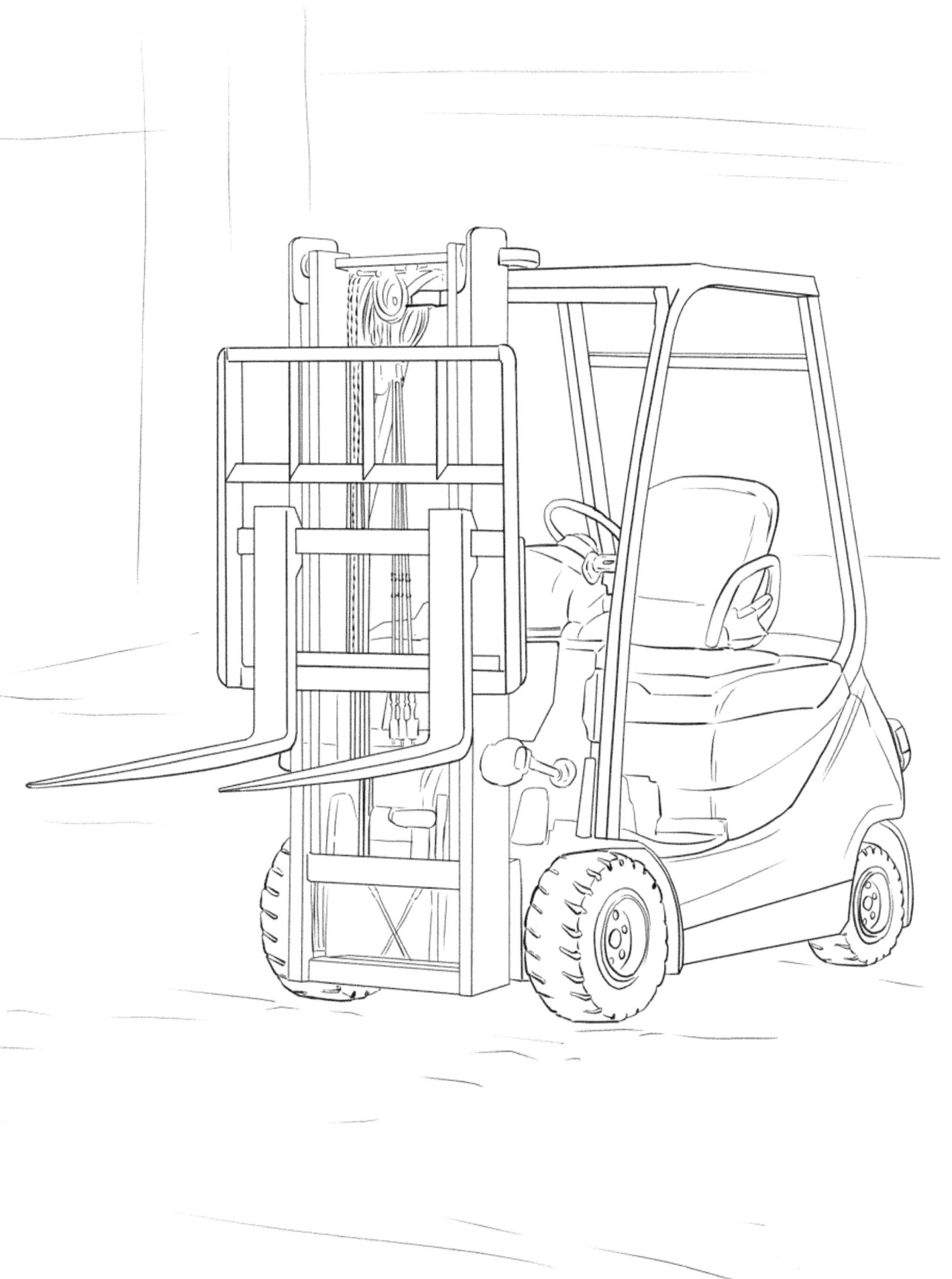

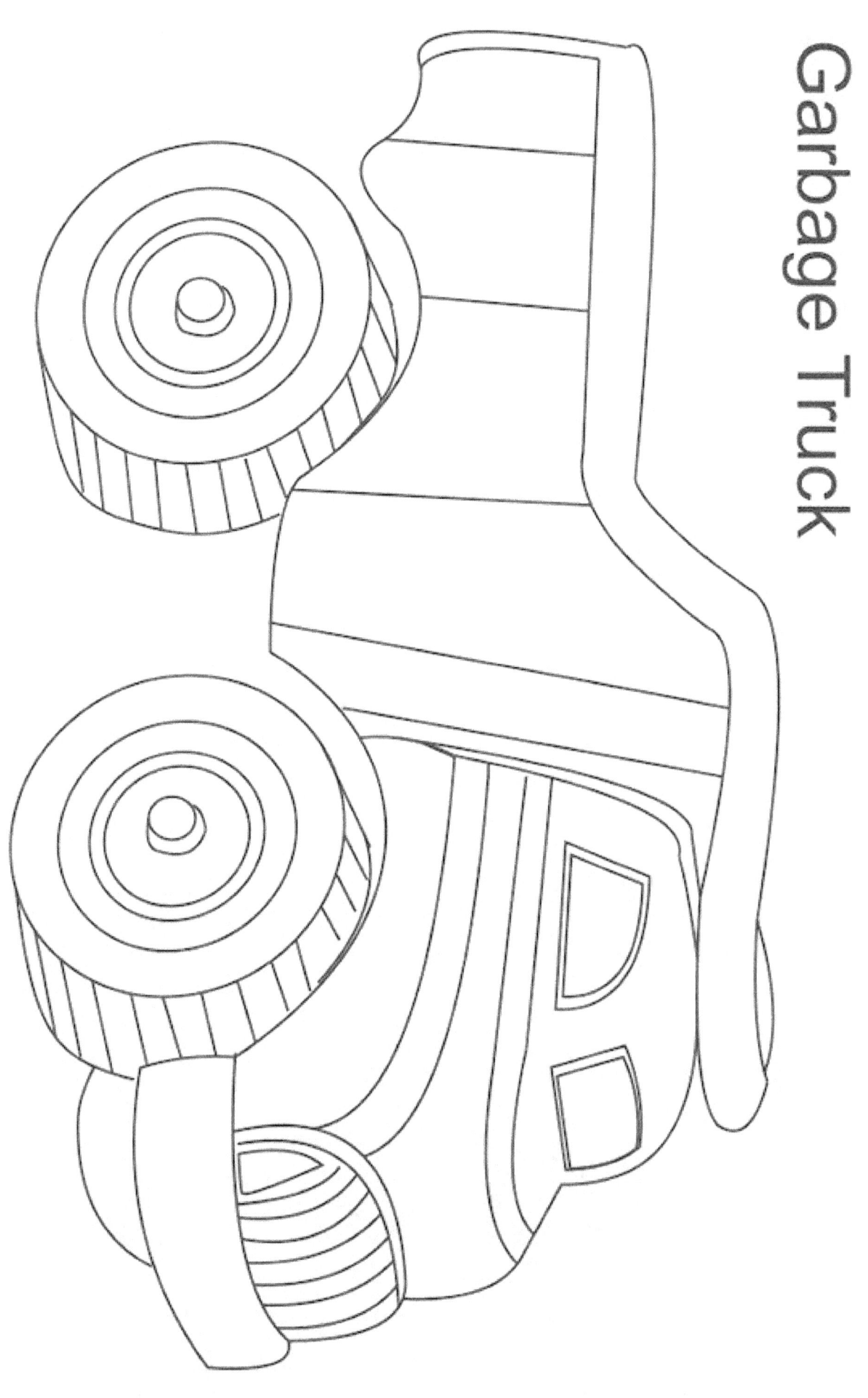

Garbage Truck

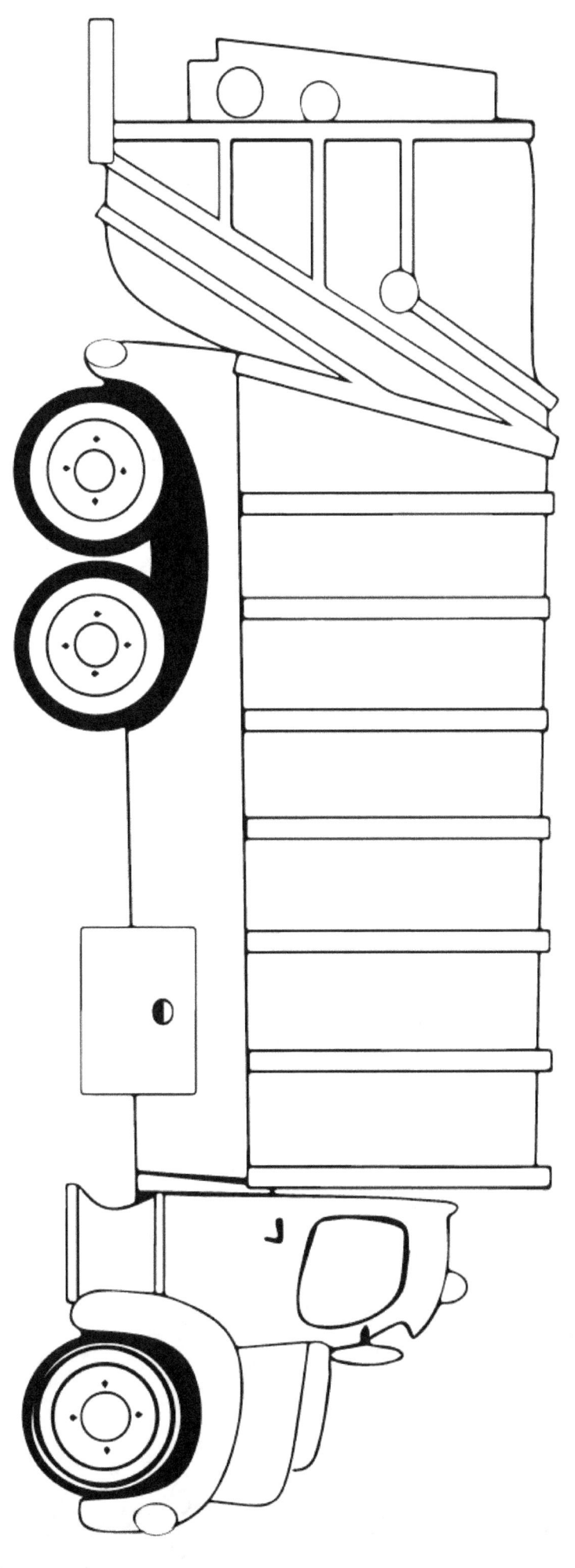

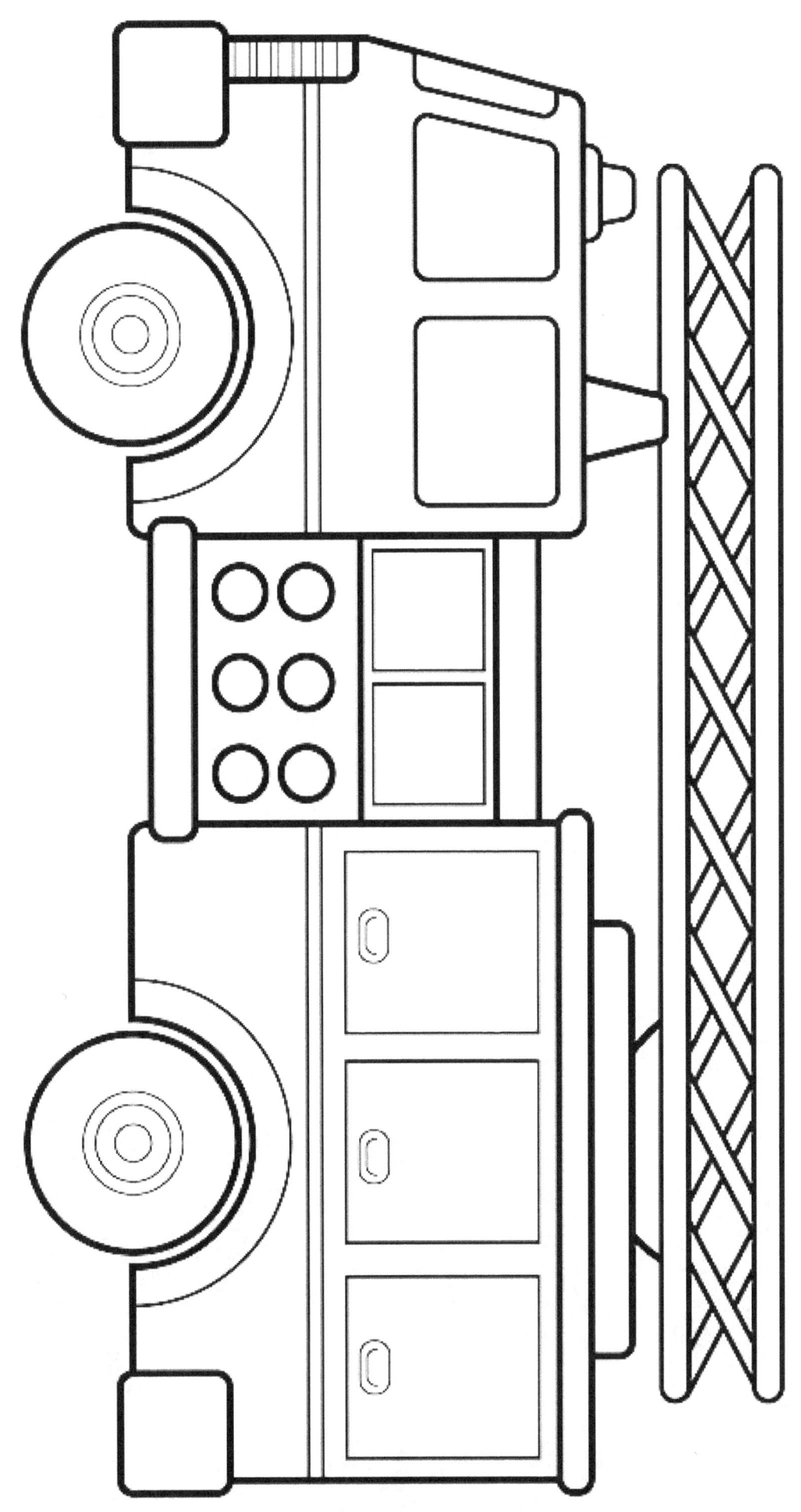

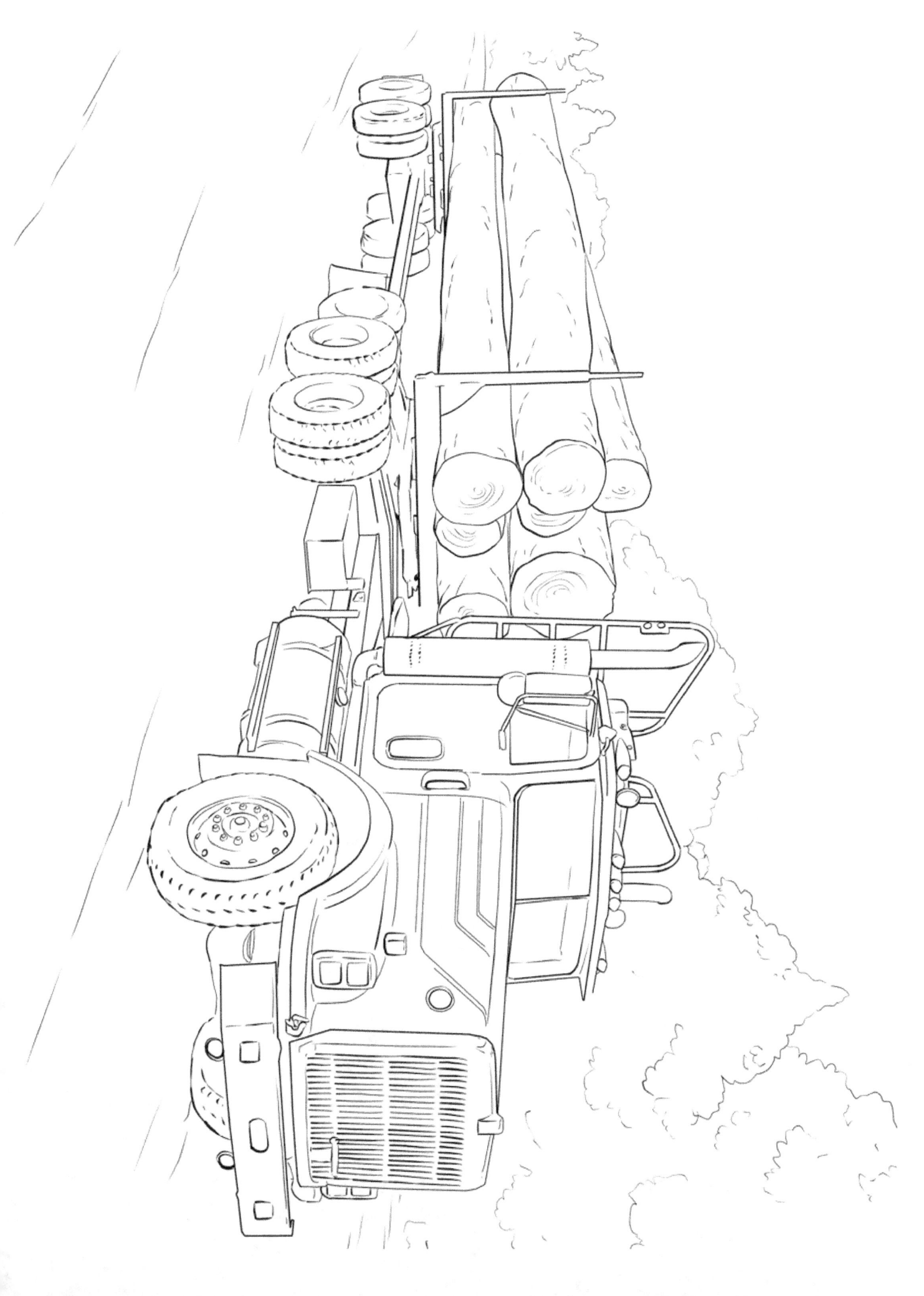

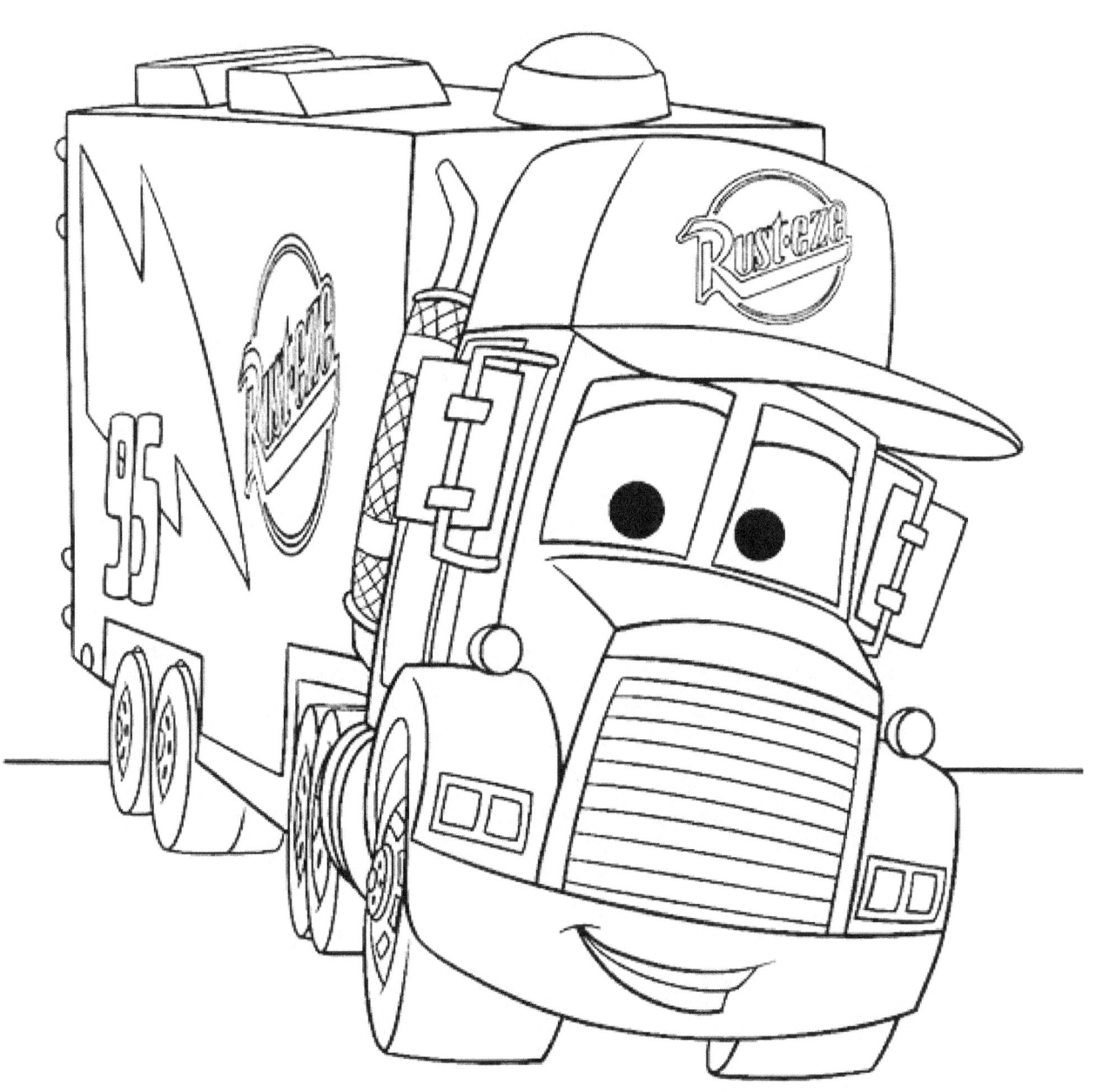

Mack

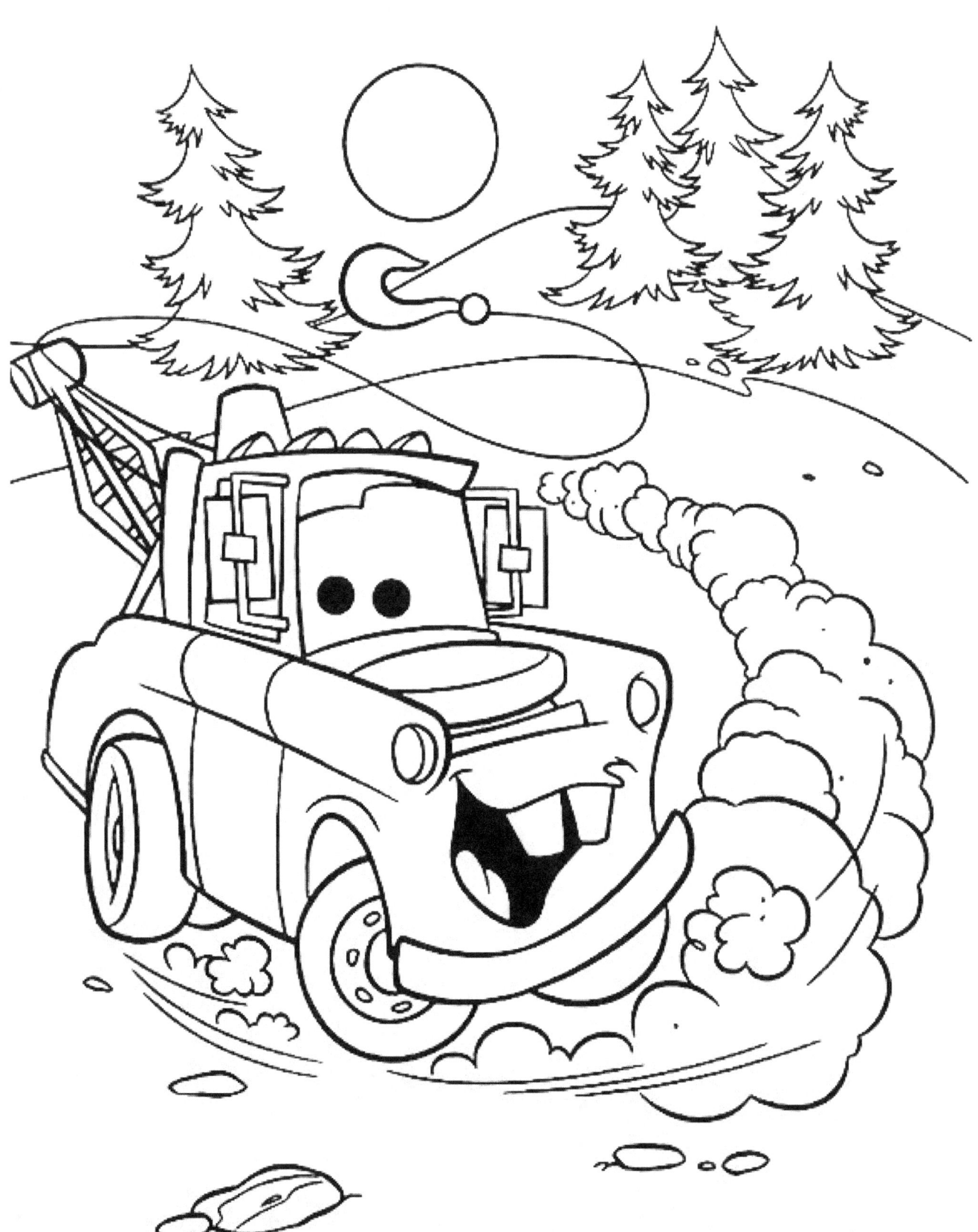

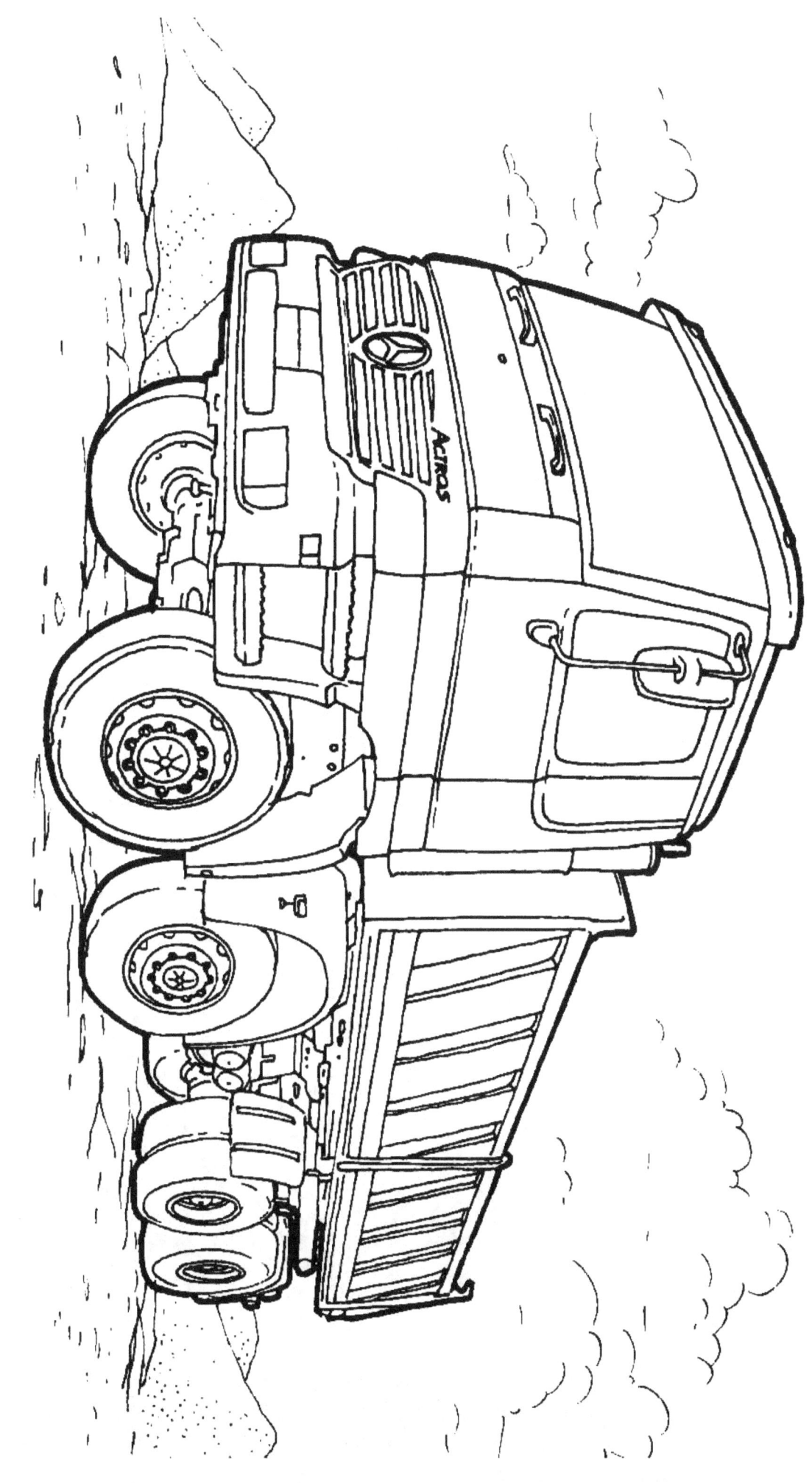

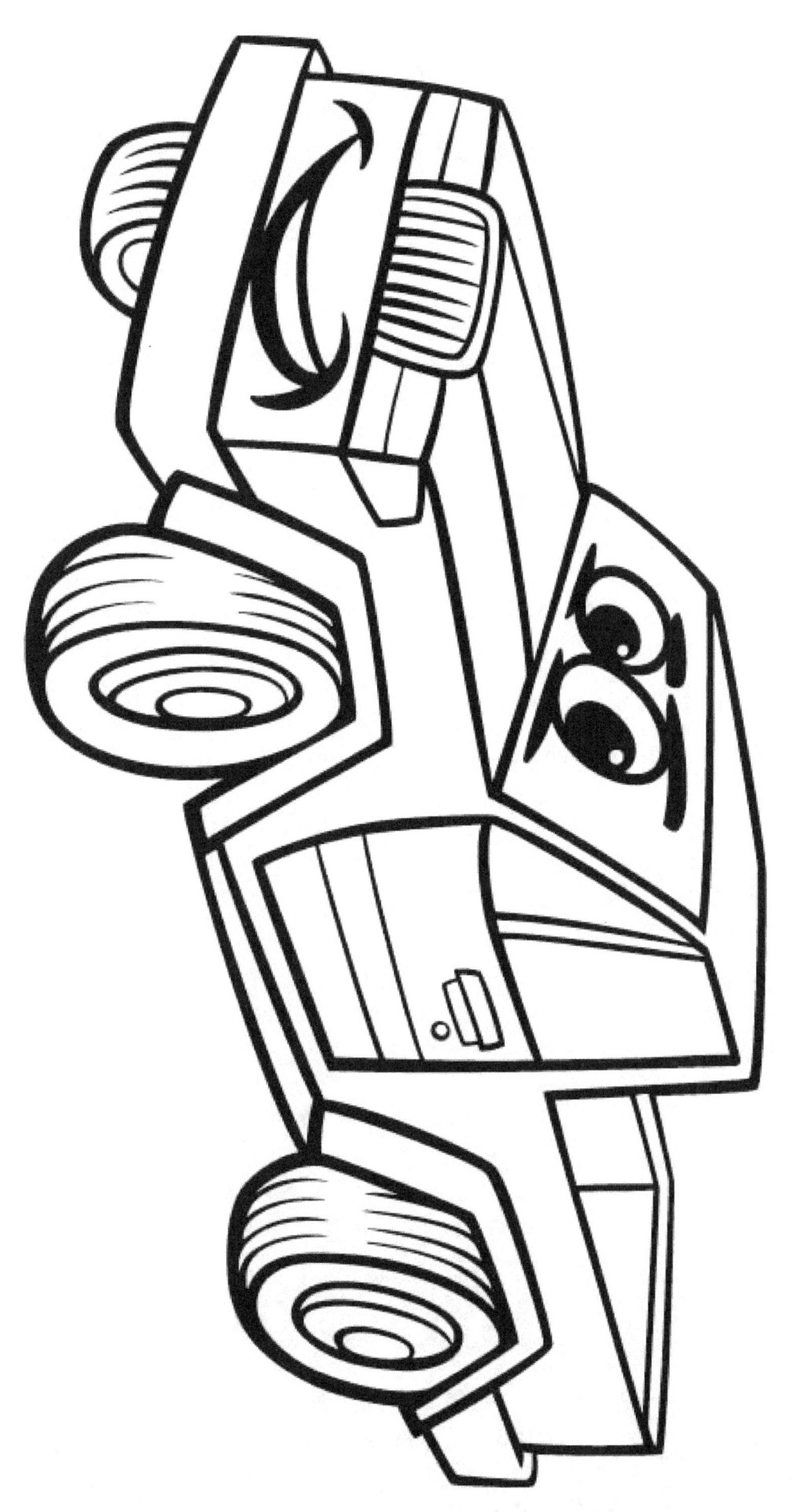

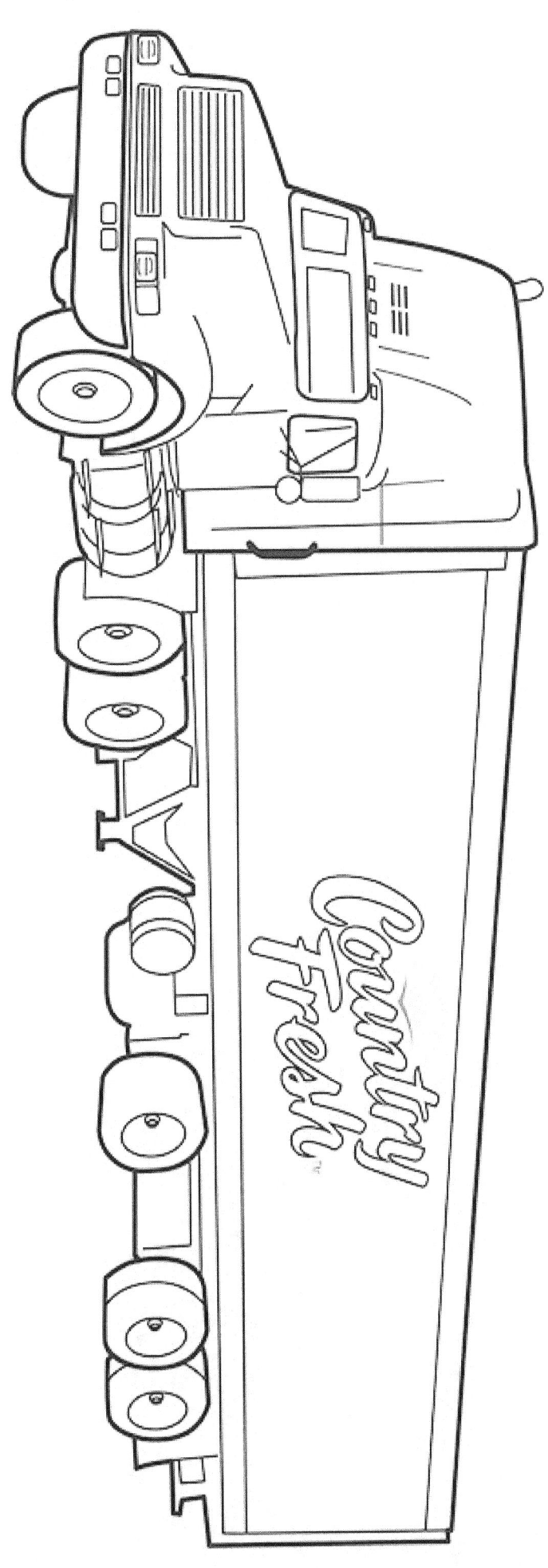

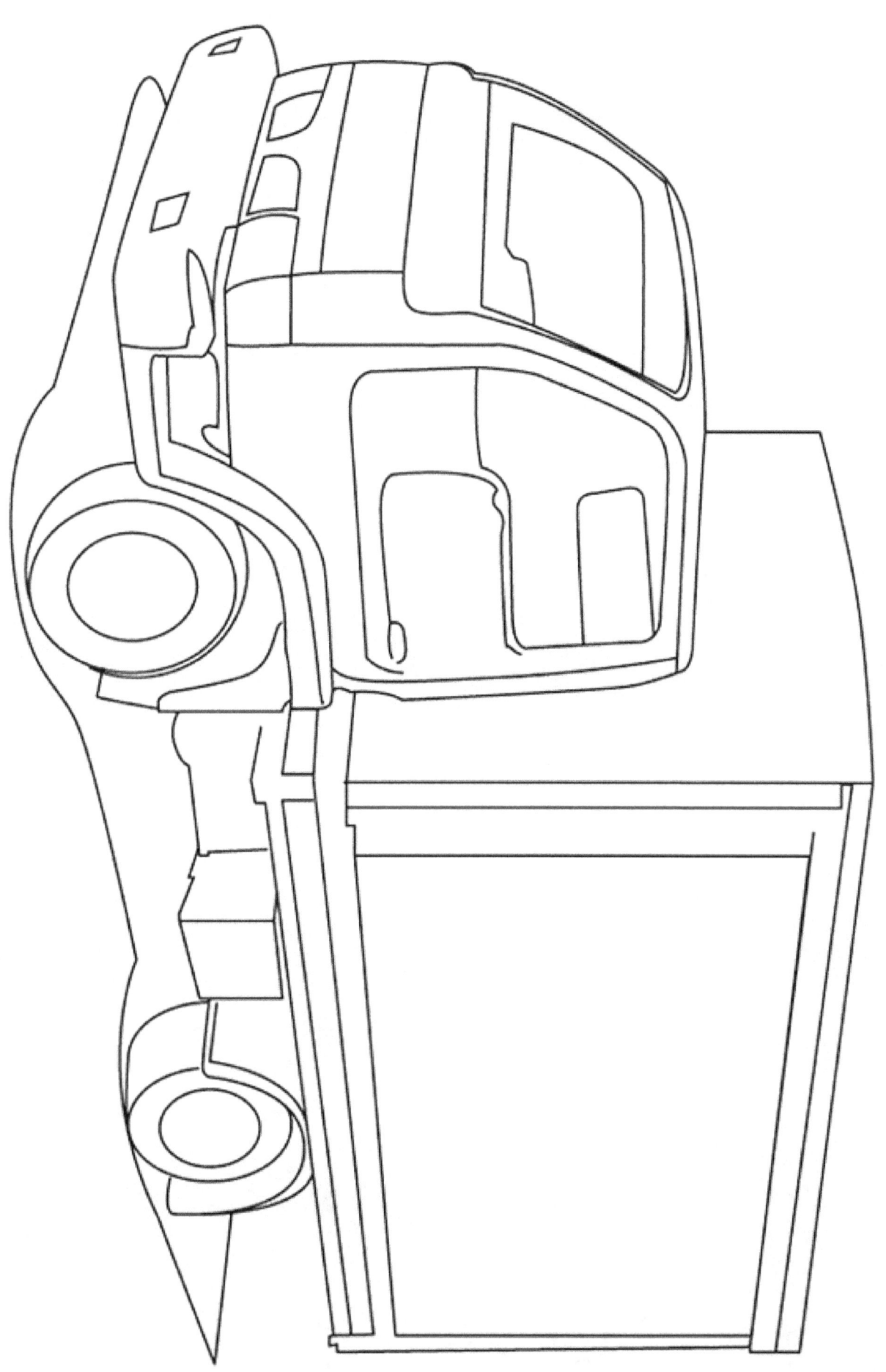

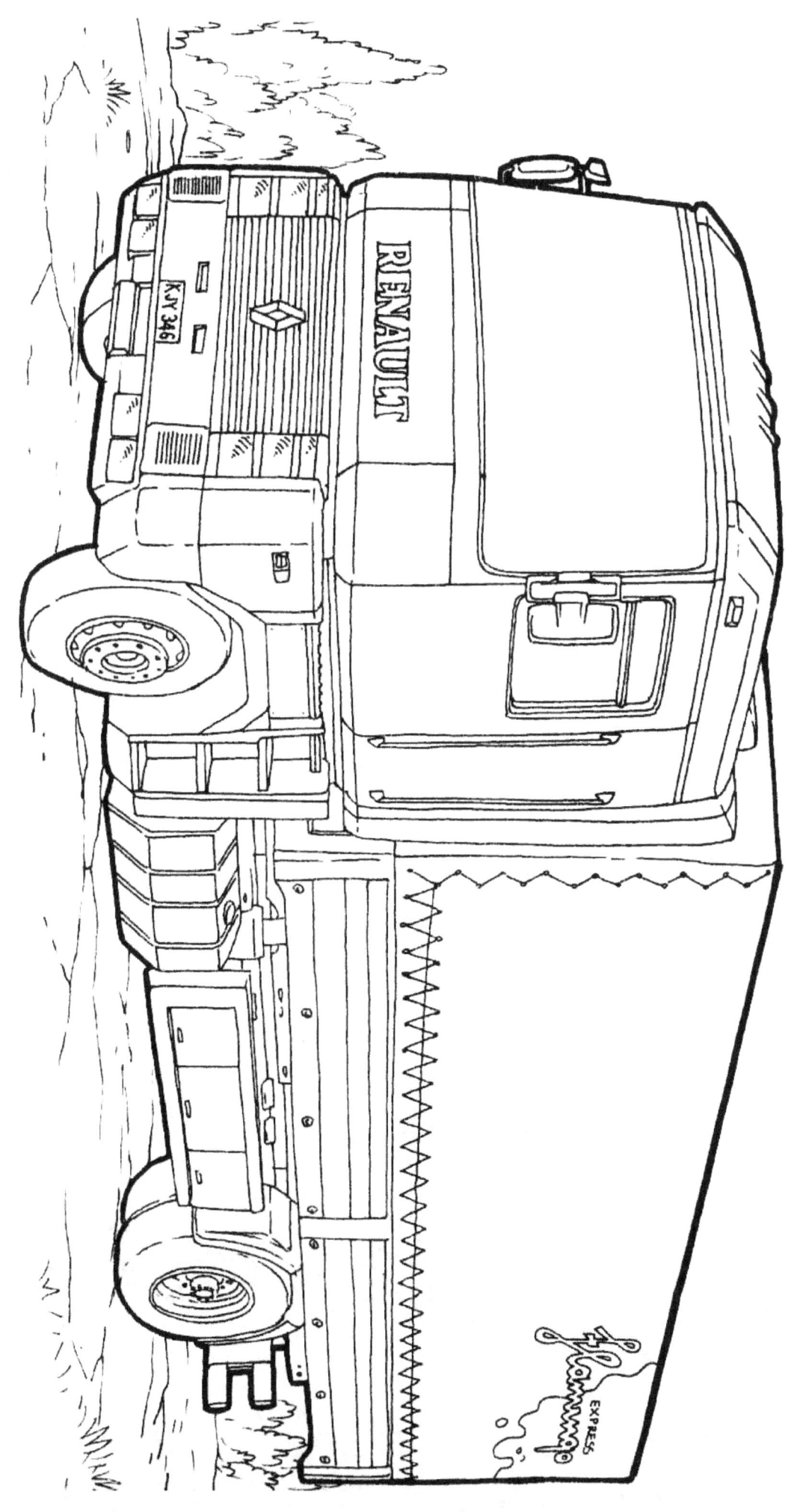

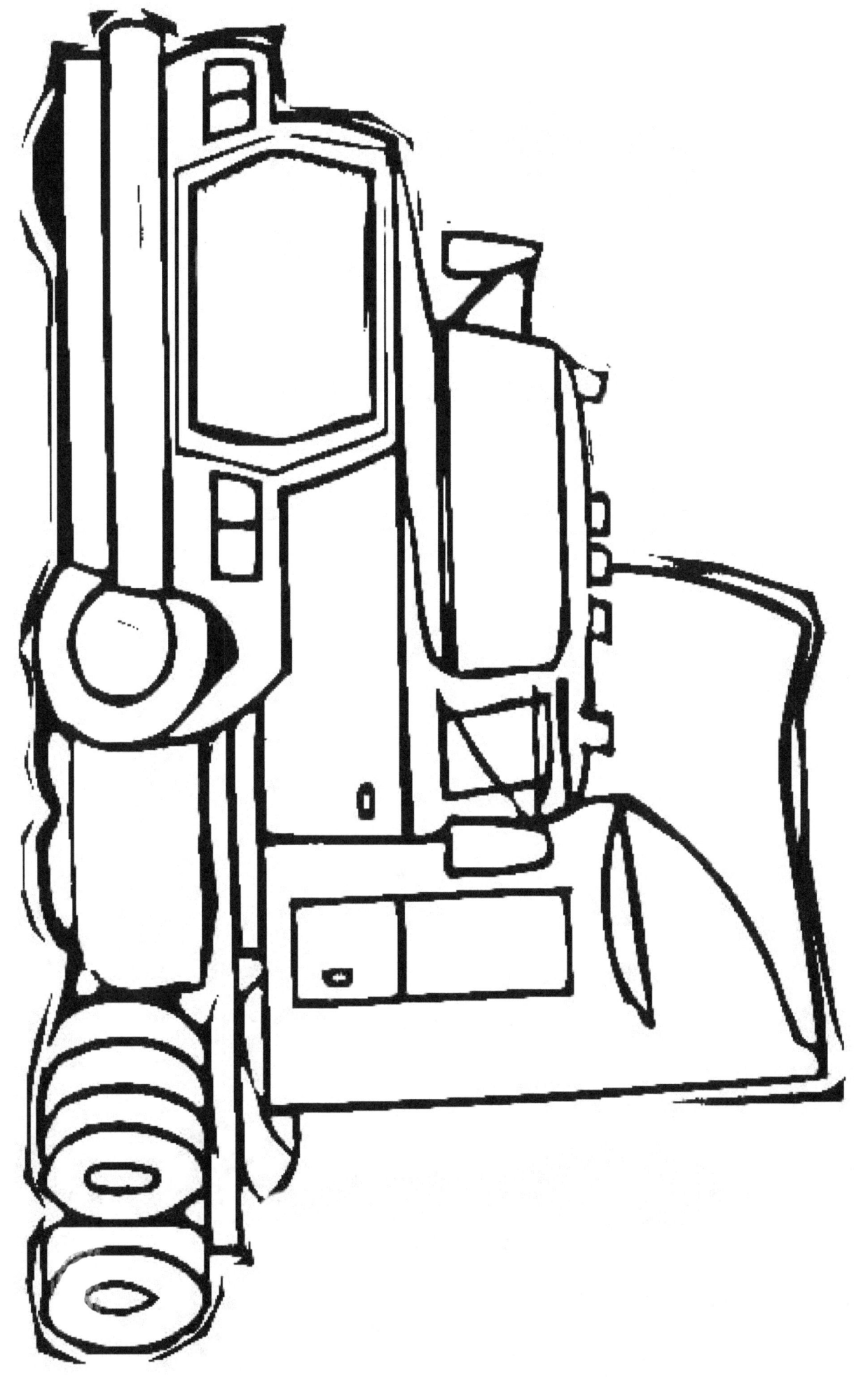

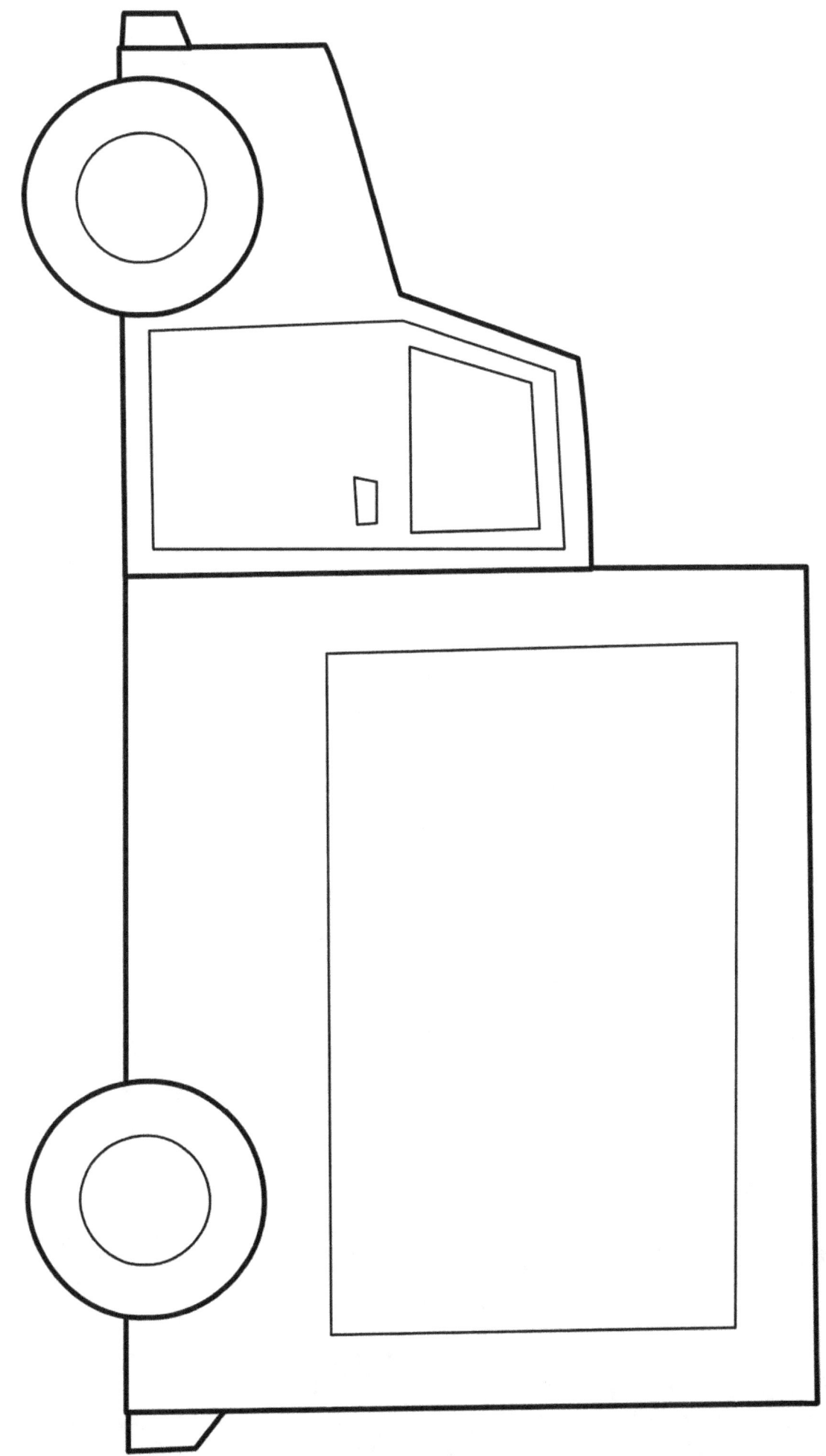

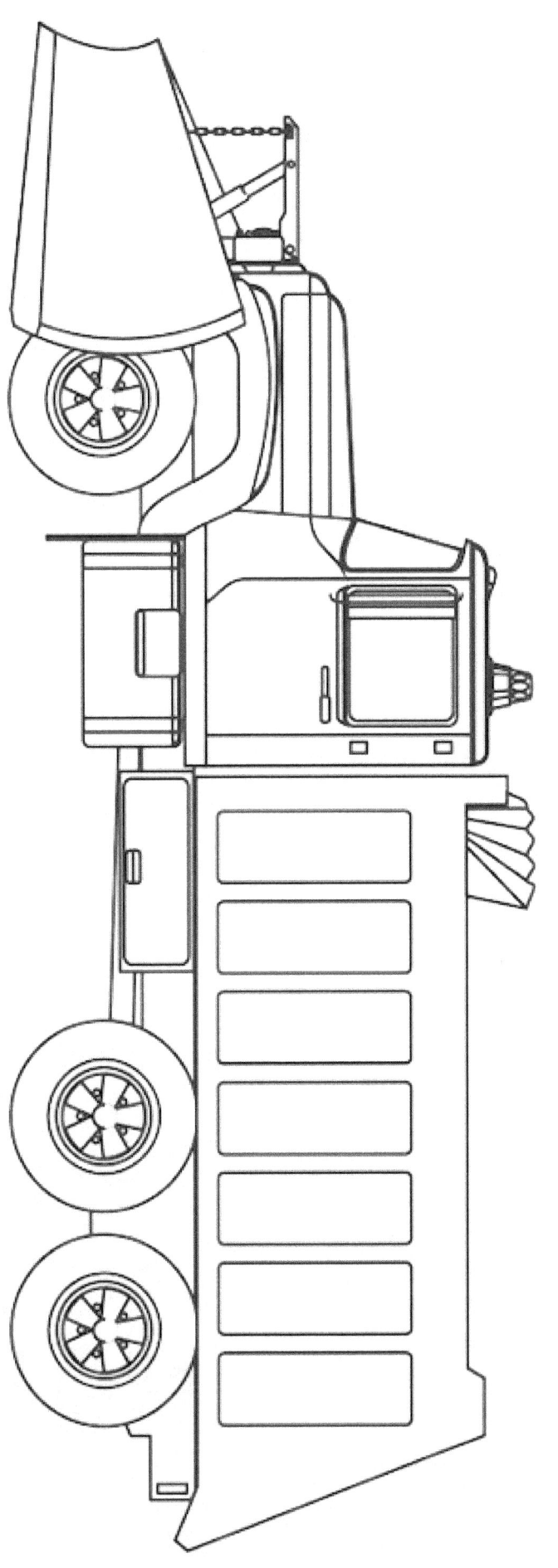

Snowplow

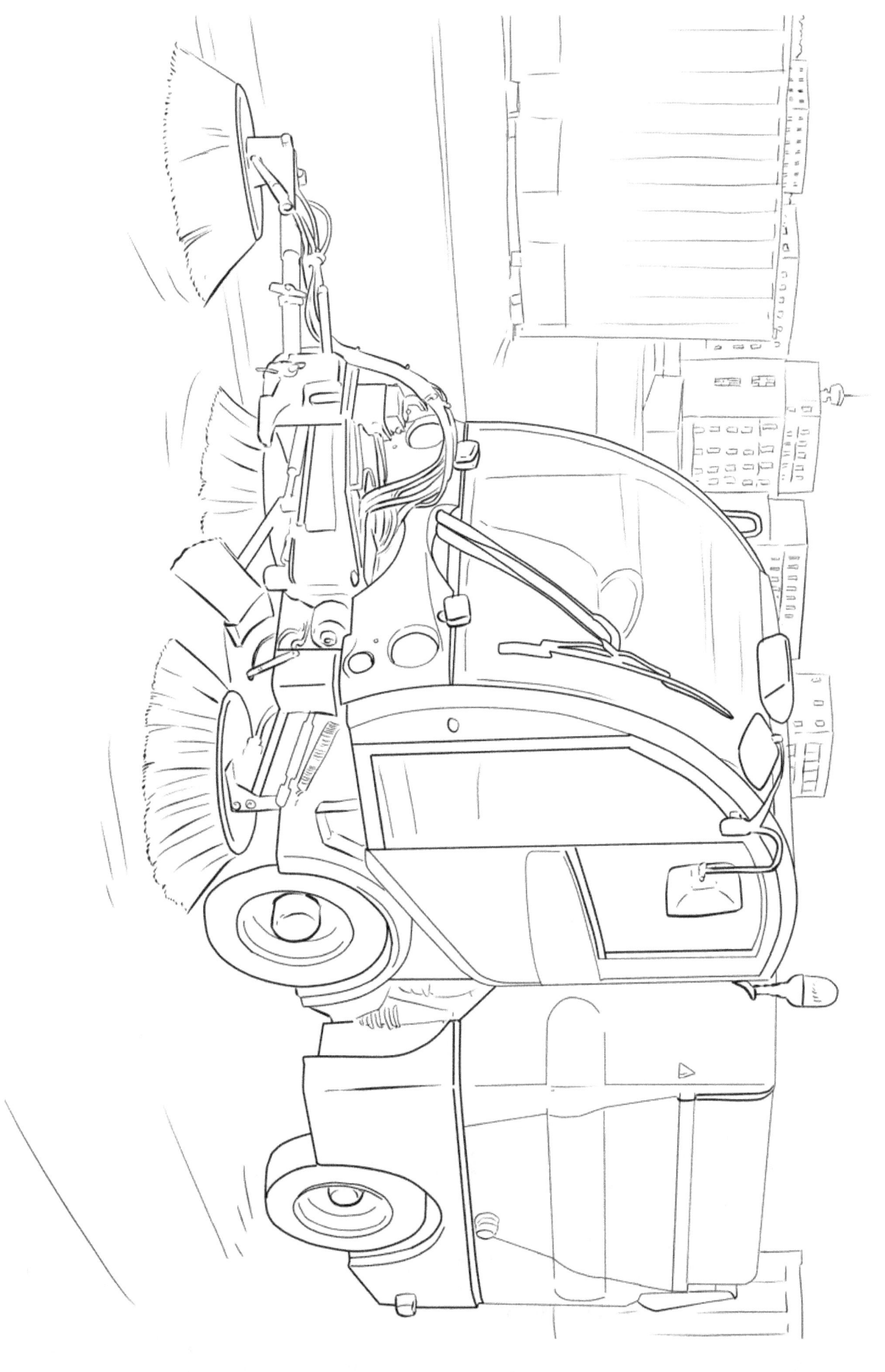

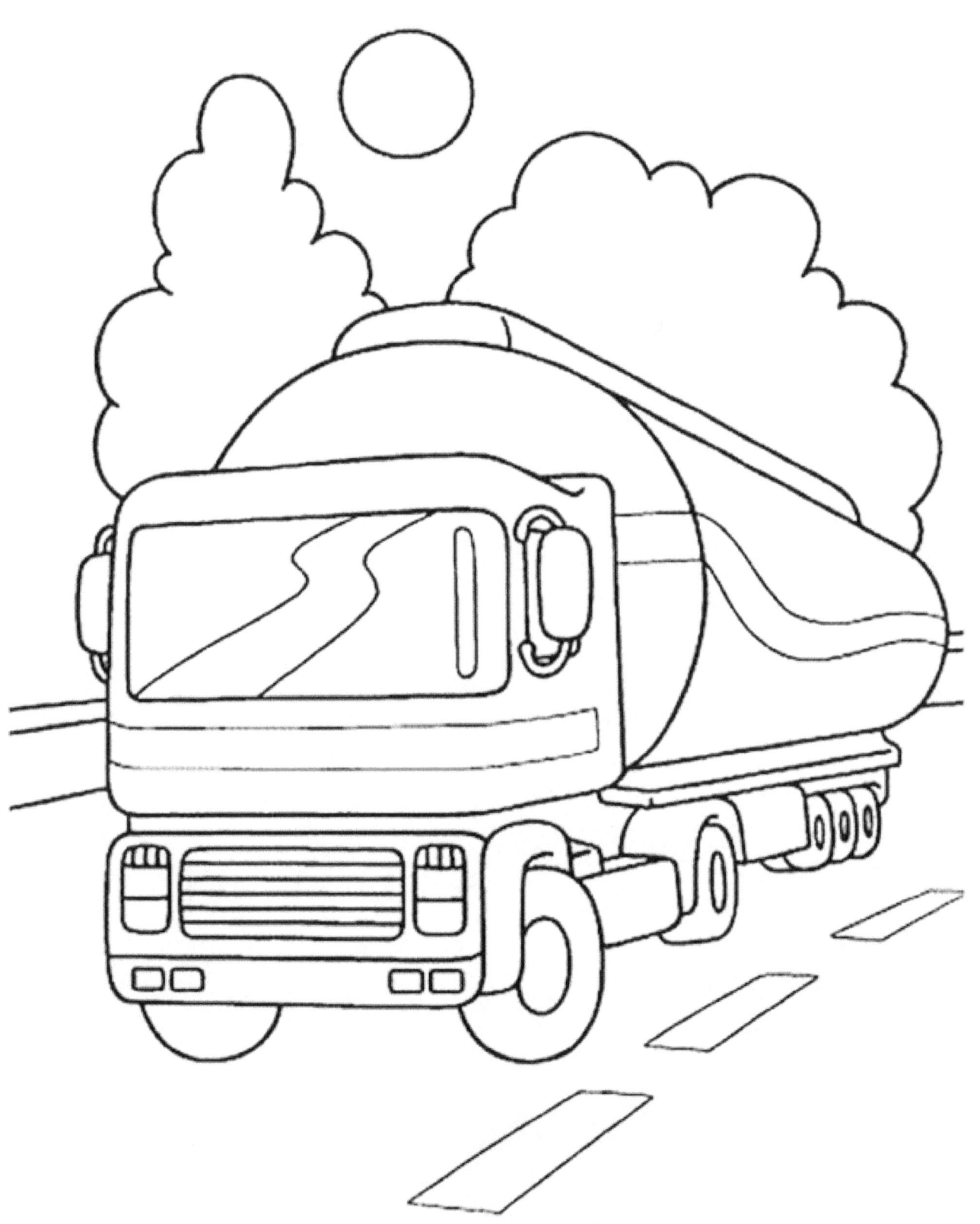

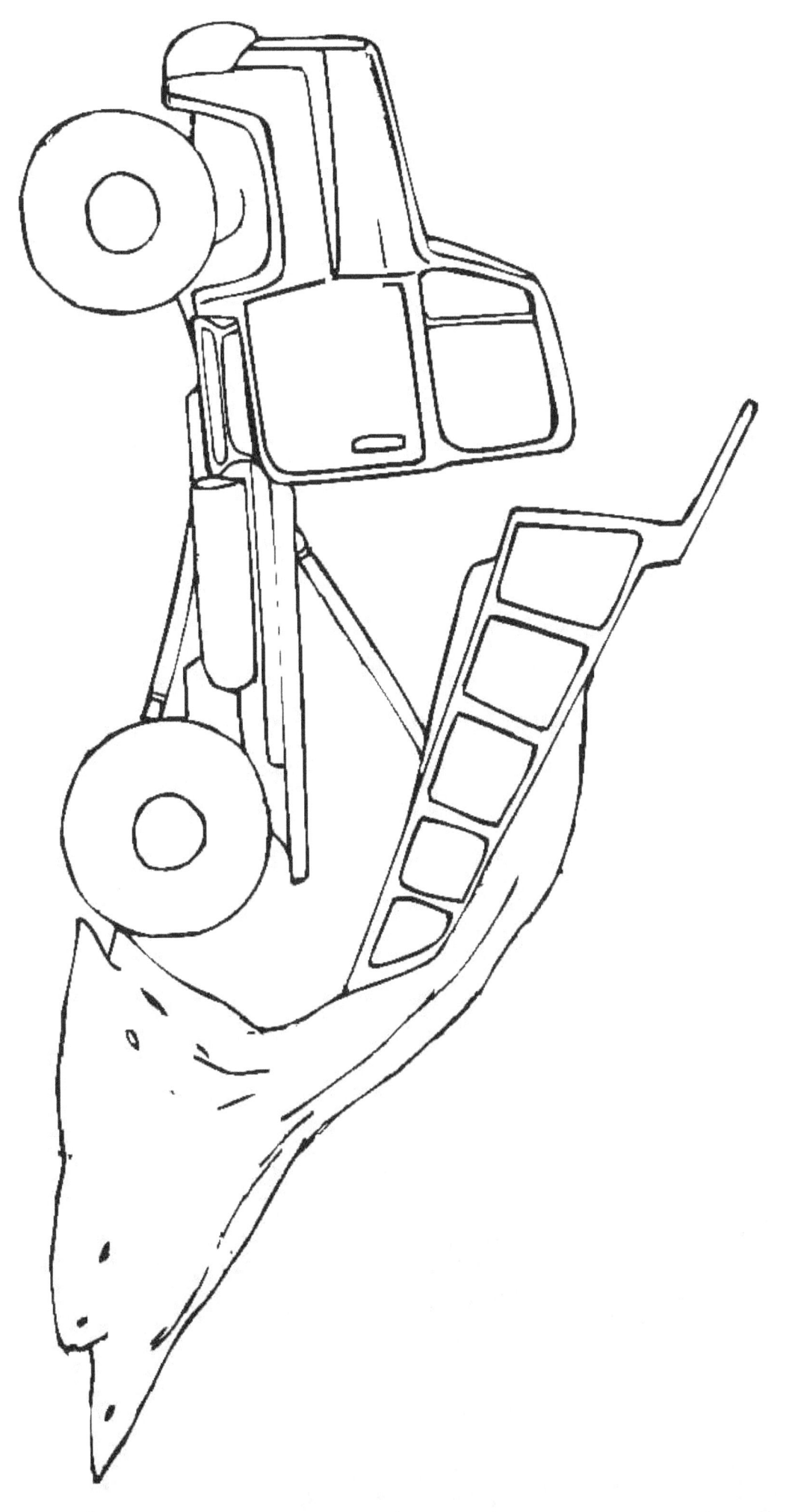

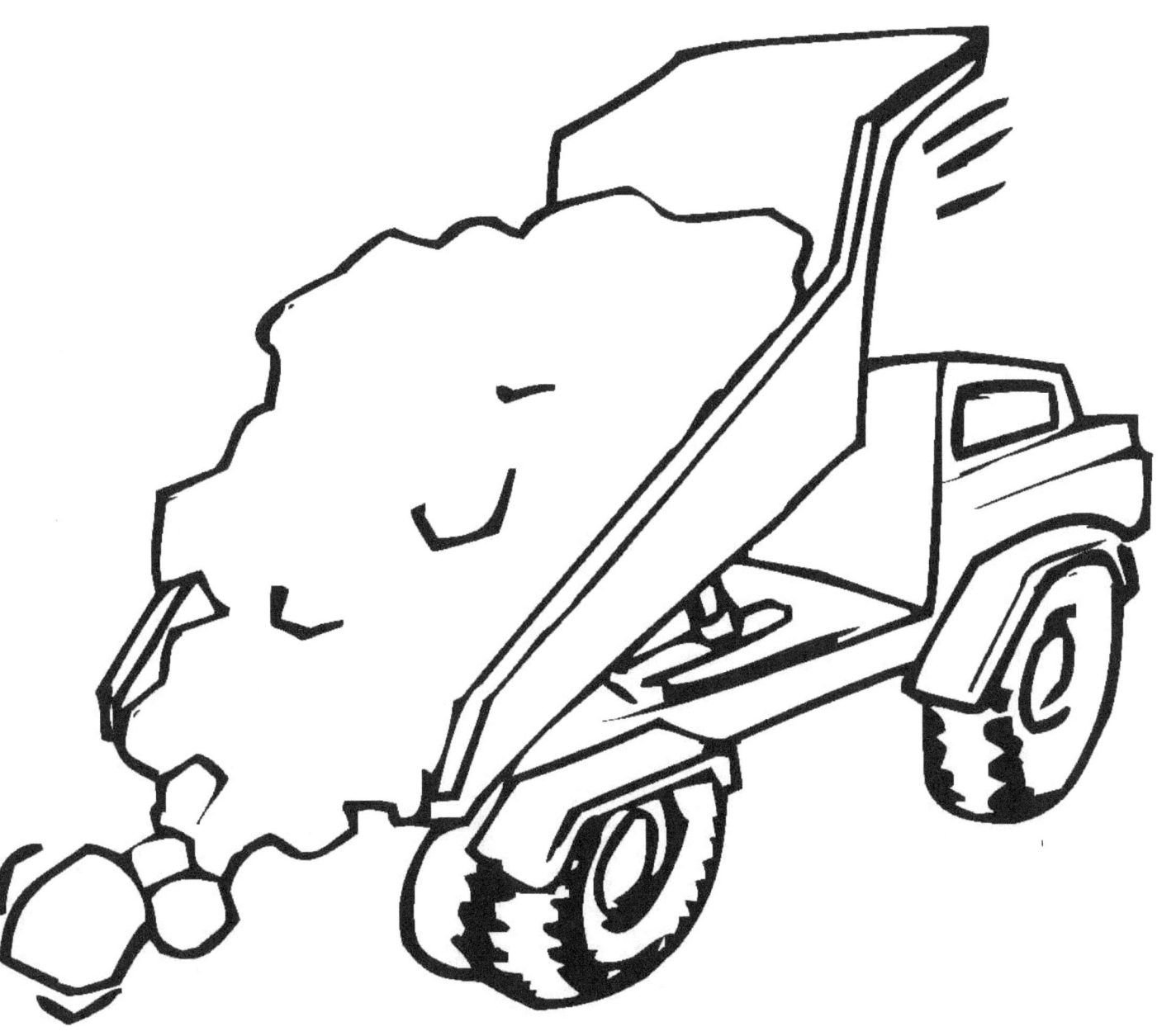

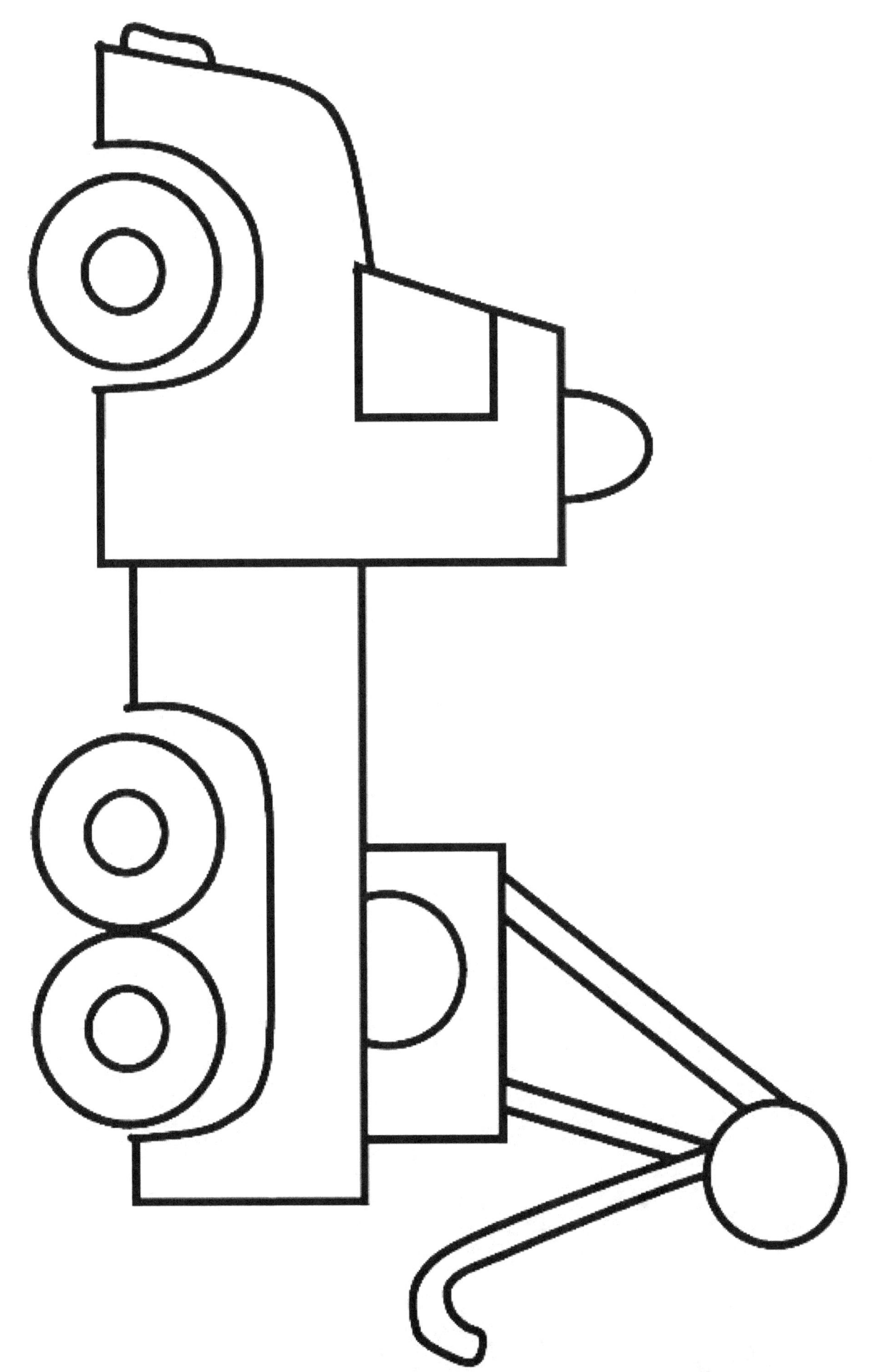

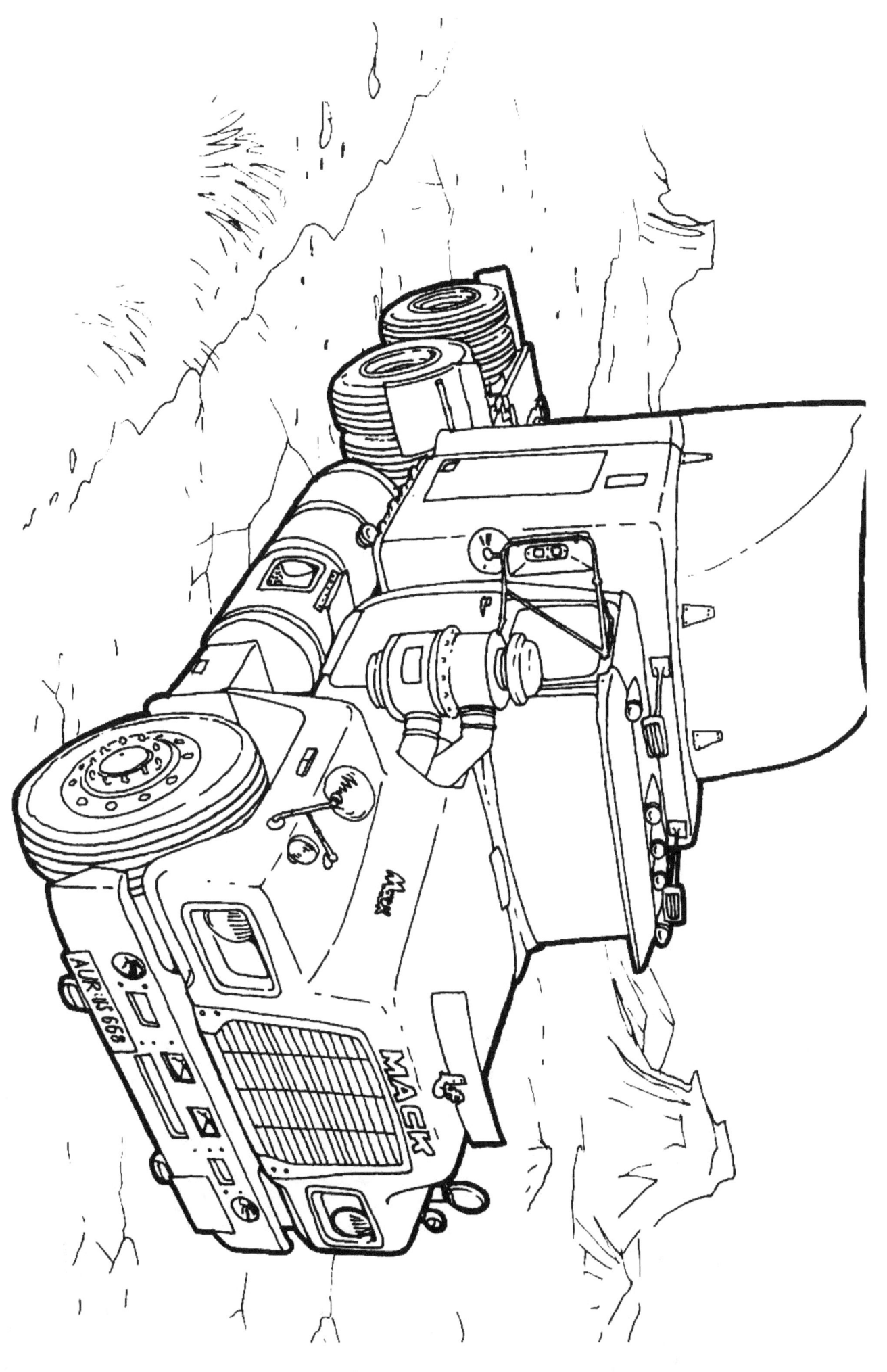

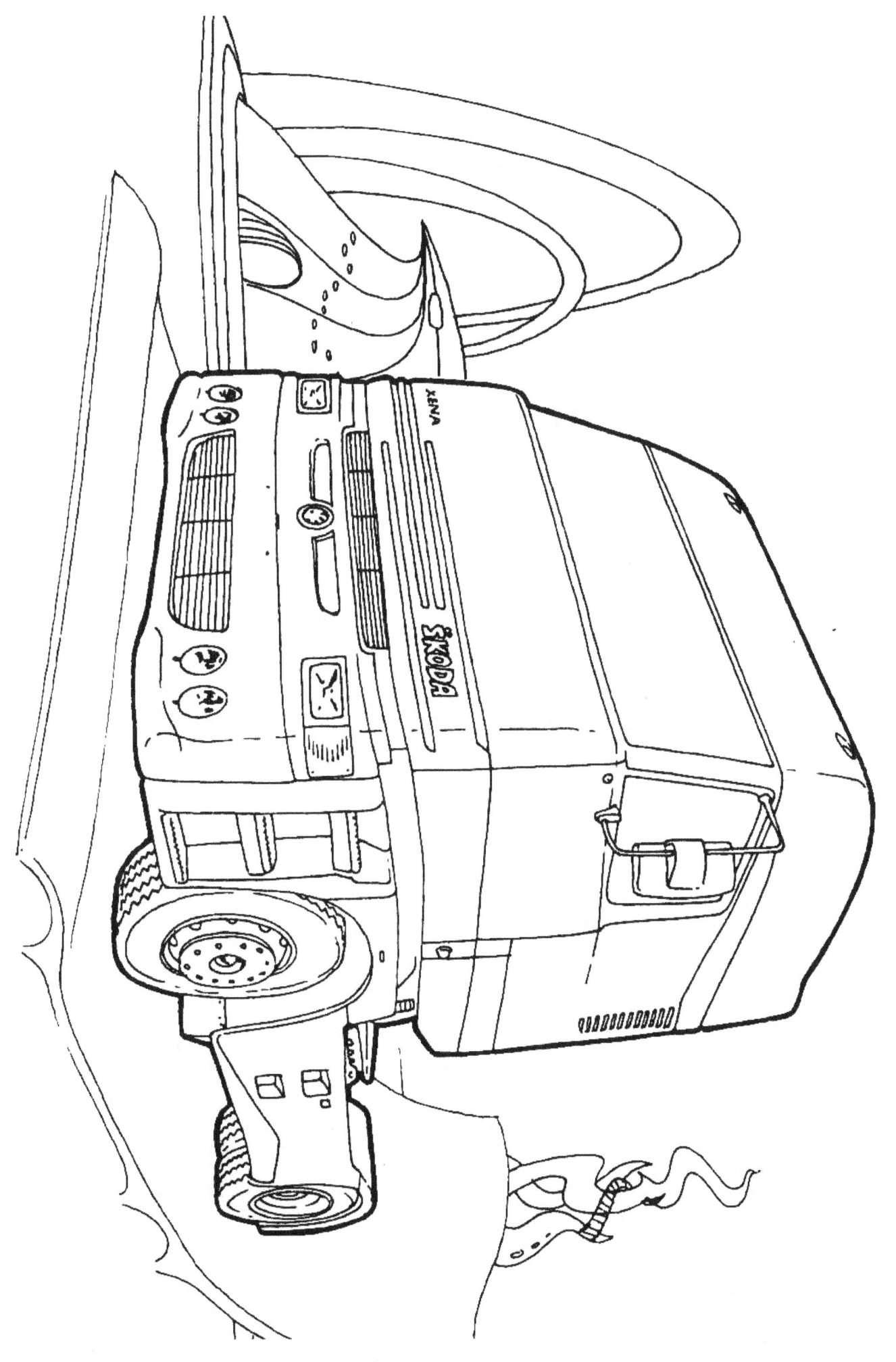

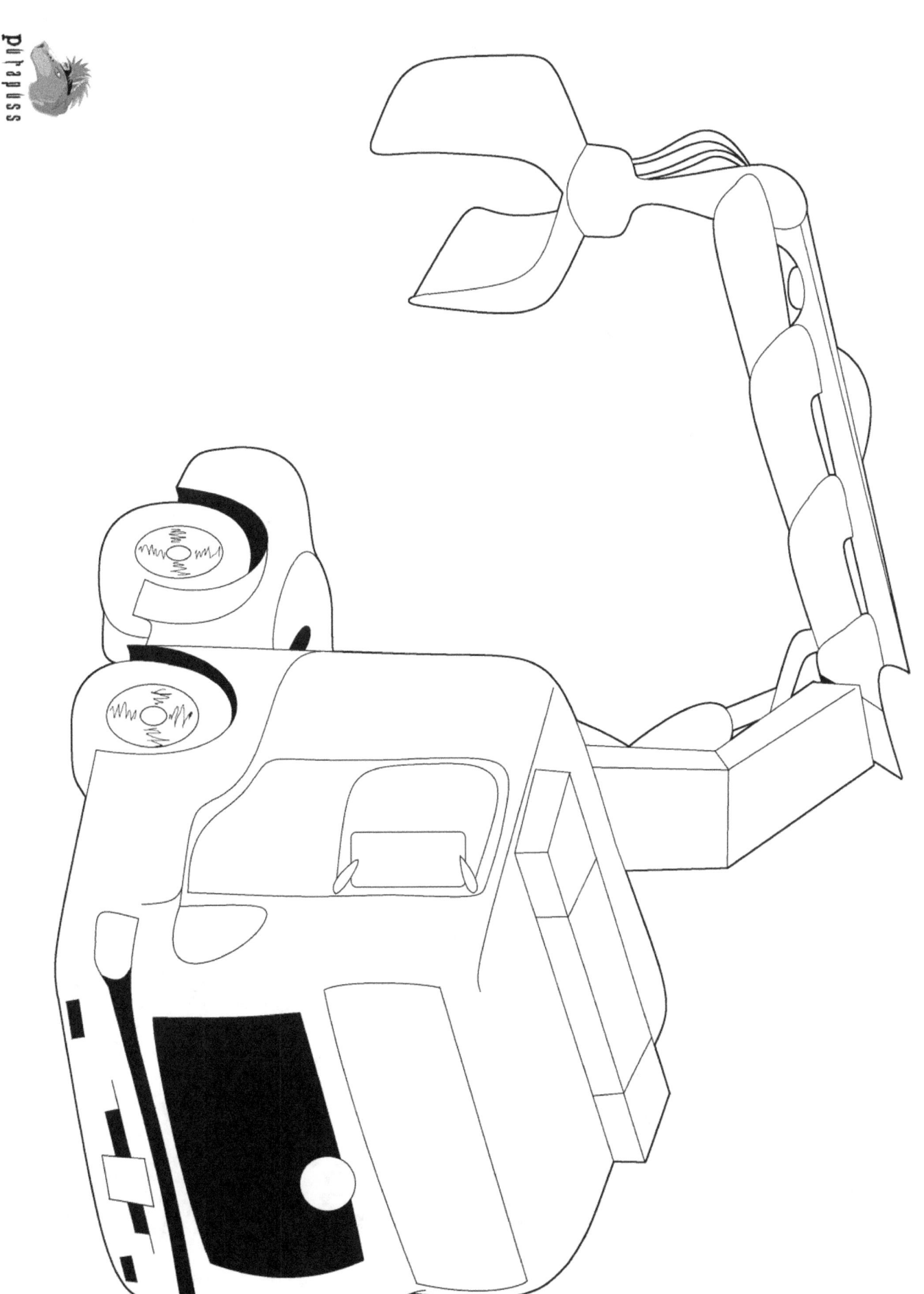

Conclusion

Thank you so much for purchasing this book. If you enjoyed it, then please leave an Amazon review. Reviews are the lifeblood for our publishing endeavors - Leaving a positive review would mean the world to us.

Cheers!
- Sunny Happy Kids

www.ingramcontent.com/pod-product-compliance
Lightning Source LLC
Chambersburg PA
CBHW081532220526
45467CB00010B/3146